UNIVERSITÄT MOZARTEUM SALZBURG

eas European Association for Music in Schools

ISME INTERNATIONAL SOCIETY FOR MUSIC EDUCATION



19 – 22 April 2017

25th EAS Conference
6th European ISME Regional Conference
in Salzburg | Austria

# JOINT (AD)VENTURE MUSIC

## Networking as a Challenge for Music Teachers

The Conference is organized by the
Department for Music Pedagogics Salzburg
of Mozarteum University Salzburg

Edited by Michaela Schwarzbauer and Elisabeth Wieland
in collaboration with Claire Austin, Juliane Friedl and Elisabeth Maria Watzl

Layout and graphic design: Ernst Blanke

**Partners**

YAMAHA | HELBLING | NAMM believe in music

LAND SALZBURG | SALZBURG CONGRESS | wissen:stadt salzburg

## Dear Delegates!

© Andreas Hauch

Welcome to Salzburg, a city with a tremendous reputation as a festival location. With the Salzburg Festival, Mozart Week, Salzburg Easter Festival and Salzburg Whitsun Festival, our city is the perfect venue for renowned artists from all over the globe.

Yet we are fully aware that these outstanding events are much dependent on a firm basis provided by people who support creativity, i.e. teachers from various types of schools, like music schools, music academies and universities. We are proud to welcome you in a city, where many 'regular' schools are offering a tremendous variety of courses appealing to young students' interest in music as well as other artistic creativity, where schools are fostering these artistic talents, for example in school choirs, school orchestras, school bands or dance companies.

Salzburg has a well-established music school, where young people regularly attend singing and instrumental lessons, where they discover the joy of making music together and in some cases even acquire competences necessary for a professional music career. Furthermore, many institutions that are responsible various forms of for teacher training have a close cooperation and a productive exchange. The Mozarteum University – a music university with an excellent reputation worldwide – is famous for bringing together musicians from all over the world.

We want to deeply thank you for vital impulses concerning the musical upbringing of a future generation and we wish you a wonderful and stimulating stay in our beautiful city.

**Dr. Heinz Schaden**
*Mayor of Salzburg*

## Dear Delegates!

As Governor of Salzburg I should like to offer a warm welcome to the participants in the regional conference of international music teachers at the Mozarteum University in Salzburg; the conference is organized jointly by the International Society for Music Education and the European Association for Music in Schools.

Salzburg is proud of its long tradition of bringing people together from all over the world in the spirit of music. I am convinced that the Baroque ambience of the old town centre of Salzburg and the unique atmosphere at the Mozarteum University will provide an inspirational setting for a rewarding exchange between music teachers from many different countries.

Allow yourself to be enchanted by the varied sounds of Salzburg! These can come from the 'Salzburg Bull', the mediaeval barrel organ which is played up on the fortress and can be heard down in the town centre, the glockenspiel in the tower of the New Residenz, street musicians, the rhythmic sounds of the horses' hooves as they draw the carriages around the cobbled streets, or the melodic sprinkling of the fountains. And do take the opportunity to enjoy at least one of the top-class concerts of classical or contemporary music.

This is the city where major music personalities in history have left behind their unmistakeable traces in sound: Paul Hofhaymer, Heinrich Ignaz Franz Biber, Georg Muffat, Michael Haydn, Leopold Mozart and above all his world famous son, Wolfgang Amadé Mozart, who was born in Salzburg. Legendary figures in music such as Herbert von Karajan, and many composers, performers as well as music teachers in more recent times, such as Cesar Bresgen, lived and worked here. This was the basis on which the world renown of the Salzburg Festival is founded and continues to evolve.

Salzburg is the home of world renowned orchestras such as the Mozarteum Orchestra, the Camerata Salzburg as well as ensembles specializing in contemporary music, for instance the OENM. Together with the Musikum Salzburg, which is concerned with providing basic music education for children of an early age, they epitomize the high standard of music education in Salzburg. All these elements make Salzburg resound in an extremely diverse manner and form the basis of its excellent reputation as a unique city of music.

In Salzburg and throughout the world music will always need attentive learners. And for this it also needs highly trained teachers who encourage talented students and convey knowledge, skill and above all joy in music. This international conference of music teachers at the Mozarteum University in Salzburg is devoted to this major concern. I wish this congress every success and I hope that all participants will enjoy a wonderful musical stay in the city and region of Salzburg.

**Wilfried Haslauer**
*Governor of Salzburg*

## Joint (Ad)venture Music

Music is omnipresent in Salzburg, the city of Mozart's birth. It is a festival city; the year starts with the Mozart Week of the International Mozarteum Foundation, then follow the Easter and Whitsun Festivals, the Salzburg Festival in summer. The Mozarteum University makes a major contribution with its International Summer Academy and the International Mozart Competition which regularly attract talented artists from all over the world to Salzburg, many of whom later enjoy highly successful careers.

We should like to offer you a very warm welcome here at the Mozarteum University in Salzburg. The title of the conference *Joint (Ad)venture Music* is not only exciting, in our opinion it is more than appropriate for the city where the renowned Salzburg Festival takes place and where there is not only a very vibrant contemporary art and music scene but also a hugely enthusiastic following for folk and traditional music. This all creates a multi-faceted sound image and one that makes the city of Salzburg unique.

The Mozarteum University in Salzburg makes a major contribution. Joint (ad)venture – for a long time already this has meant a university with three main sectors in which the departments of drama and the visual arts are a considerable enrichment alongside the many varied instrumental classes, as well as training for music teachers. Perhaps the sometimes provocative, energetic activities of our budding actors and actresses are needed to contrast or complement the meticulously followed sphere of fostering Mozart which of course constantly has to be revitalized.

Bringing together what superficially appears to be incompatible, I have in mind here for instance the wonderful cooperation between our tuba class and the dancers of the Carl Orff Institute. Besides performances by participants in our instrumental classes, the opera institute, our symphony orchestra, which are of course characterized by the aim to attain professionalism, they make up a major integral part of life at our university. We extend an important invitation to our students of music education at the Mozarteum to become familiar with this variety and to provide a firm basis for specific didactic and methodical approaches.

Students should have the opportunity to shape joint (ad)ventures in the integration of opera performances, and in creating educational concepts in teaching music. Joint (ad)ventures also need a solid basis of theoretical knowledge so as not to lose the ground beneath one's feet. A further essential aspect of our work is research and a well-founded academic training; publications from our institution contribute an added dimension to our educational aims.

When you enter our building, the encounter between human beings, the continuous interaction between representatives of the most varied cultures appear to be a very important aspect which exemplifies above all that joint adventures require trust and tolerance.

We have confidence in the training we provide for prospective music teachers. Training in this sphere is especially important because it ensures that in the future we will continue to have fantastic musicians as well as enthusiastic audiences.

For an institution such as the Mozarteum University in Salzburg, major conferences are of course an adventure in themselves, a logistical challenge, an interaction of many separate elements that hold our institution together. The organizers of this conference have certainly already encountered some adventurous situations in the course of planning. Adventures have to be approached with excitement, curiosity as well as openness for the unexpected.

We are very pleased that this congress can be followed worldwide via live streaming (first introduced at the Mozarteum in 2016).

We wish all participants this spirit of 'allowing oneself to be surprised' for the entire conference and are grateful to all those who have shown the courage to embark on this adventure.

**Sarah Wedl-Wilson**
*Deputy-Chancellor for External Relations*



Translation: Elizabeth Mortimer

## Dear Delegates, Dear Guests – Herzlich Willkommen!

On behalf of the Organizing Team of the 25$^{th}$ EAS Conference and the ISME Regional Conference I welcome you warmly here at Mozarteum University Salzburg. We are very delighted to host a conference which enables pedagogues, teachers and researches from all over the world to share knowledge gained, good practice examples and – last but not least – visions concerning the future of music education in schools.

Here at Mozarteum University Salzburg in the heart of Salzburg where talents mature into artistic personalities music teacher training at a high level is regarded as a fundamental need: Music educators in schools and in non-curricular fields will be the guarantors for the advancement of young musicians but even more for the establishment of an interested and open minded audience in the future.

Joint ventures are part of everyday life at our university: meeting points between artistic fields, scientific fields, pedagogical fields are established and get enriched by cultural activities from without. A fine network of inspiration and cooperation makes it possible for our department specialized in music teacher training to foster the development of joint (music) adventures for people of all ages.

The EAS Conference is focusing on music in schools, on the vital challenge of offering music education to as many young people as possible, supported by the strong belief that that accesses to a joint adventure music should be open to everybody.

We hope that this Conference is going to be a fantastic adventure for all of you and that new joint ventures are going to be initiated. We look forward to hosting you here in Salzburg and wish you all a stimulating and enjoyable conference with long lasting impressions.

**Monika Oebelsberger**
*Head of the Department for Music Pedagogics*
*at Mozarteum University Salzburg*

## Dear Delegates!

©Foto Hofer

On behalf of the board of the European Association for Music in Schools (EAS) I am delighted to welcome you to the 25th EAS Conference/ the 6th ISME European Regional Conference.

After two conferences in Vienna (1991 and 2003) this is now the third EAS-conference in Austria, a country in the middle of Europe with a rich musical tradition and high quality music education. We are looking forward to meeting in the beautiful and culturally rich city of Salzburg at the Mozarteum University Salzburg, an institution with 500 teachers and a strong worldwide reputation both in historically and today.

In a way the EAS is still in 'celebration mode': 2015 saw the 25th anniversary of the EAS, and now we celebrate the 25th EAS conference. Our association's conference has developed over the years to become the most important annual meeting for music education in schools at a European level. At this 2017 conference we are happy to welcome colleagues from nearly all European countries, and beyond. We also celebrate the 15th EAS Student Forum which offers students the opportunity to engage in exchange of ideas and musical resources. This is our small but, we believe, important contribution to the very important idea of involving the next generation of music educators in our network. Over the years, around 400 young people have been involved in these fora; many of them are now advanced music teachers in schools, some are music teacher trainers and two already support our network as EAS National Coordinators. Therefore we particularly welcome the participants of the International EAS Student Forum, but also all other students who join this conference, including the doctoral students of the 7th EAS Doctoral Student Forum.

Both the EAS board, which will be newly elected – by all members – at the General Meeting in Salzburg, and the EAS National Coordinators meet prior to the conference. This year we are also honoured to welcome the executive board of the International Society for Music Education (ISMF) which also meets in Salzburg at the same time.

In noting the broad range of activities surrounding these annual events, it becomes clear that the EAS conferences are key to the development and strengthening of our music education network. As a "joint@venture", which is also the main focus of this conference, it will be exciting to exchange ideas about "networking as a challenge for music educators" and to explore ways in which we can take the work of the EAS further into the music education world. Aside from the keynotes; workshops; school visits; practice, research and poster presentations; we hope that the break times, the evenings, and the conference dinner will provide opportunities for further discourse. Discussions about music education inevitably involve the exploration of cultural values and encourage tolerance and openmindedness: all very important in this time of political upheaval.

I would like to thank Monika Oebelsberger and her conference team for the enormous commitment and energy which has made this event possible, and I wish you all a stimulating and enjoyable conference!

**Gerhard Sammer**
*President of EAS*

## Dear Delegates!

Welcome to Salzburg and to the EAS 2017 conference. This event is one of the International Society of Music Education's (ISME) regional conferences and we are proud to be partnering with you once again. As an organization that supports and promotes the breadth of music education worldwide, ISME's members consistently surprise me with their dedication and commitment in the pursuit for an excellent, inclusive, and equitable environment where music dialogue and practice can take place. Our focused commissions and forum help shape international conversation around such topics as policy, special education, community music, early childhood, and educating the professional musician. The special interest groups reflect timely themes such as health and wellbeing, spirituality, Sistema, and popular music. ISME also provides development grants; our work currently includes projects in Africa, Pakistan and India. New initiatives include the development of a book series with Routledge, advancing towards an ISME foundation, and deepening our relationship with the NAMM foundation. There is of course our biennale conference next held in Baku, Azerbaijan in July 2018. This event reflects a commitment in supporting music educators in the Turkic region and we hope to see many of you there. As the President of ISME I hope you all find your (ad)venture in the days to come. Enjoy your time in Salzburg exploring new horizons with fellow adventures as you continue your musical journey.

**Lee Higgins**
*President of ISME*

# ORGANIZING COMMITTEE

Prof. Dr. Monika Oebelsberger
Ass.Prof. Andreas Bernhofer, PhD

MMag. Bakk. Art. Katharina Anzengruber
Gisela Deutschmann
Juliane Friedl
Lisa Grüneis
Univ. Ass. Mag. Helmut Schaumberger
Ao. Prof. Dr. Michaela Schwarzbauer
Univ. Ass. Mag. Elisabeth Wieland, MA
Elisabeth Watzl

# STUDENT FORUM

Sen. Lect. Dr. Marina Gall (University of Bristol)
Prof. Dr. Oliver Krämer (Rostock University of Music and Drama)
Dr. Branka Rotar Pance (University of Ljubljana)
Jonė Girdzijauskaitė (Lithuanian Academy of Music and Theatre)
Lisa Grüneis (Mozarteum University Salzburg)

# DOCTORAL STUDENT FORUM

Prof. Dr. Thade Buchborn (Hochschule für Musik Freiburg)
Prof. Dr. Mary Stakelum (Bath Spa University)

# SCIENTIFIC BOARD

Prof. Dr. Thomas De Baets (LUCA School of Arts, Leuven)
Ass.Prof. Andreas Bernhofer, PhD (Mozarteum University Salzburg)
Prof. Dr. Thade Buchborn (Hochschule für Musik Freiburg)
Dr. Natassa Economidou Stavrou (University of Nicosia)
Mag. Dr. Erik Esterbauer (Mozarteum University Salzburg)
Sen. Lect. Dr. Marina Gall (University of Bristol)
Prof. Dr. Rûta Girdzijauskiene (Klaipeda University)
Ass. Prof. Dr. Anna Houmann (Malmö Academy of Music)
Mag. Dr. Anna Maria Kalcher (Mozarteum University Salzburg)
Prof. Dr. Oliver Krämer (Rostock University of Music and Drama)
Ass. Prof. Ene Kangron (Estonian Academy of Music and Theatre Tallinn)
Prof. Mag. Dr. Christoph Khittl (University for Music and Performing Arts Vienna)
Prof. Dr. Isolde Malmberg (Rostock University of Music and Drama)
Prof. Dr. Monika Oebelsberger (Mozarteum University Salzburg)
Prof. Dr. Gerhard Sammer (University of Music Würzburg)
Ao. Prof. Dr. Michaela Schwarzbauer (Mozarteum University Salzburg)
Prof. Dr. Mary Stakelum (Bath Spa University)
Doc. Dr. Sc. Sabina Vidulin (University of Juraj Dobrila in Pula)
Adri de Vugt (University of the Arts The Hague)
Prof. Dr. Christopher Wallbaum (Music University, Leipzig)

**Acknowledgements**
We would like to express our gratitude to all institutions and companies whose generous support has helped us to make this conference possible.

# CONTENTS

# PRE-CONFERENCE SCHEDULE (CLOSED MEETINGS)

## MONDAY, APRIL 17

17:00 - 19:30 **EAS-Board Meeting** (Chair: Gerhard Sammer)
Mozarteum University Salzburg, Paris-Lodron-Straße 9, ROOM: Dachgeschoss

## TUESDAY, APRIL 18

09:00 - 17:00 **EAS Board Meeting**
Mozarteum University Salzburg, Mirabellplatz 1, ROOM: 1010

14:30 - 18:30 **EAS Doctoral Student Forum (DSF)** (Chairs: Mary Stakelum & Thade Buchborn)
KunstQuartier, Bergstraße 12a, Salzburg

17:00 - 18:30 **Meeting of ISME Executive Board and EAS-Board** (Chairs: Lee Higgins & Gerhard Sammer)
Mozarteum University Salzburg, Mirabellplatz 1, ROOM: 2048

17:00 - 19:00 **EAS Student Forum (SF)** (Chairs: Branka Rotar Pance & Oliver Krämer)
Mozarteum University Salzburg, Paris-Lodron-Straße 9, ROOM: Dachgeschoss

19:00 **Social Evening with International buffet of SF/DSF/EAS Board/ISME ExBoard**
Mozarteum University Salzburg, Mirabellplatz 1, ROOM: Students' Lounge

## WEDNESDAY, APRIL 19

09:00 - 12:00 **EAS Board Meeting**
Mozarteum University Salzburg, Mirabellplatz 1, ROOM: 1010

09:00 - 16:00 **National Coordinators' (NC) Meeting** (Chair: Natassa Economidou Stavrou)
Mozarteum University Salzburg, Mirabellplatz 1, ROOM: 2048

09:00 - 17:30 **EAS Student Forum (SF)**
Mozarteum University Salzburg, Paris-Lodron-Straße 9, ROOM: Dachgeschoss

09:00 - 17:00 **EAS Doctoral Student Forum (DSF)**
KunstQuartier, Bergstraße 12a, Salzburg

# CONFERENCE SCHEDULE

## WEDNESDAY, APRIL 19

09:00 - 12:00 **School Visits (register in advance)**
Meeting point: FOYER, Mozarteum University Salzburg, Mirabellplatz 1

13:00 - 17:30 **Registration**
Mozarteum University Salzburg, Mirabellplatz 1, ROOM: Solitär

15:45 - 17:30 **Musical City-Tour in Salzburg**
Meeting point: FOYER, Mozarteum University Salzburg, Mirabellplatz 1

**18:00 - 19:30 OPENING CEREMONY with Music**
Mozarteum University Salzburg, Mirabellplatz 1, ROOM: Solitär

**Welcome Addresses**
Dr. Wilfried Haslauer (Governor of the Federal Province of Salzburg)
Dr. Heinz Schaden (Mayor of Salzburg)
Sarah Wedl-Wilson, MA (Deputy-Chancellor of Mozarteum University Salzburg)
Prof. Lee Higgins (President of ISME)
Prof. Dr. Gerhard Sammer (EAS President)
Prof. Dr. Monika Oebelsberger (Head of the Department for Music Pedagogy at Mozarteum University Salzburg)

**Music**
**"(Im)Possible Music"**
Andreas Hofmeir and his Tuba-Class of Mozarteum University Salzburg
Recorder-Consort of Mozarteum University Salzburg

**19:30 - 20:30 Wine reception**

# THURSDAY, APRIL 20 | 8:45 – 14:00

08:45 **Morning (AD)VENTURE: ROOM "Solitär"**

09:00 **KEYNOTE: Susan O'Neill (CAN)**
**Exploring a "Learning Lives" Approach to Connection and Collaboration in Music Education**
Chair: Monika Oebelsberger (AUT) | ROOM: "Solitär"

10:00 **BREAK**

| | PARALLEL-SESSIONS | | |
|---|---|---|---|
| | **ROOM "Bösendorfersaal"**<br>PRESENTATIONS<br>Chair:<br>*Marie-Francoise Quinet (FRA)* | **ROOM "Hörsaal"**<br>PRESENTATIONS<br>Chair:<br>*Ruth Frischknecht (CHE)* | **ROOM 2046**<br>PRESENTATIONS<br>Chair:<br>*Andreas Bernhofer (AUT)* |
| 10:15 | *Wolfgang Kosmata (AUT), Rob Bolland (NLD)*<br>"Helden von heute – Falco Goes School" | *Daniel Fiedler, Daniel Müllensiefen (GER)*<br>Musical Trajectories and Creative Orientation of Music Lessons Affect the Development of Interest in 'Music' in Secondary School Students | *Seyhan Bulut (TUR)*<br>The Function of Instrument Masters' Video Lessons in Conservatory Education |
| 10:45 | *Sabina Vidulin (CRO)*<br>The Collaboration between School, Music Associations and Town Institutions: What Does a Student Acquire? | *Julia Getino, Assumpta Valls, Cristina González-Martín (ESP)*<br>Pupils and Composers: From Listening to Contemporary Music to Musical Creation in the Classroom | *Kenneth Liske (USA)*<br>Arts-Integrated Instruction: Curricular Innovation for Pre-Service Educators and University-School-Community Partnerships |
| 11:15 | COFFEE BREAK | | |
| | **ROOM "Bösendorfersaal"**<br>**PRiME Special Focus Group**<br>PRESENTATIONS<br>Chair:<br>*Isolde Malmberg (GER)* | **ROOM "Hörsaal"**<br>PRESENTATIONS<br>Chair:<br>*Richard Hallam (GBR)* | **ROOM 2046**<br>PRESENTATIONS<br>Chair:<br>*Sabina Vidulin (CRO)* |
| 11:30 | *Thade Buchborn, Elisabeth Theisohn (GER)*<br>"Was our Song Already Good?" Criteria-Based Processes of Composing Music in School | **Yamaha-Session:**<br>*Fritz Höfer (AUT)*<br>New Forms of Teaching and Learning in Piano Teaching Thanks to the Integration of Digital Techniques: Yamaha Discpiano Enspire and Yamaha TransAcoustics | *Dale Misenhelter (USA)*<br>Pre-Service Teacher Perceptions of Interdisciplinary Teaching |
| 12:00 | *Jonas Völker (GER)*<br>Multicultural Music Learning with Percussion Instruments: A Design-Based Research Study | *Smaragda Chrysostomou (GRC)*<br>User Generated Content (UGC) Environments Fostering Collaboration to Enrich Music Teaching in Schools | *Jelena Martinovic Bogojevic (MNE)*<br>A National Project Supporting the Development of Music Pedagogy in Montenegro |

12:30 **LUNCH**

**"Meet the EAS Board Candidates" (12:30 – 13:15) | ROOM: "Foyer"**

**CONCERT (12:45 & 13:15): Chor & Band BORG Gastein (BORG Bad Hofgastein)**
**ROOM: "Kleines Studio"**

| PARALLEL-SESSIONS | | | |
|---|---|---|---|
| **ROOM 2047**<br>PRESENTATIONS<br>Chair:<br>*Gerhard Sammer (GER)* | **ROOM 2048**<br>PRESENTATIONS<br>Chair:<br>*Anna Houmann (SWE)* | **ROOM 2049**<br>WORKSHOP<br>Chair:<br>*Carola Schormann (GER)* | |
| [Practice Paper] *Clara Horbach (GER)*<br>Music and Movement with Unaccompanied Refugee Minors | [Research Paper] *Fanny Chung (HKG)*<br>Interdisciplinary Approaches for Music Learning in Hong Kong | [Workshop] *Francis Dubé, Astrid Marin, Jean-Philippe Després (CAN)*<br>Designing Non-Digital Music Mini-Games WITH and FOR Students | 10:15 |
| [Practice Paper] *Lili Schutte (NLD)*<br>It Takes Two to Teach Music | [Practice Paper] *Michaela Weinhauser, Franziska Böhm (GER)*<br>A Body-Oriented Constructivist Approach to Music Learning: Exploring Different Metres and Rhythm Polyphony through Movement, Voice and Instruments | | 10:45 |
| COFFEE BREAK | | | 11:15 |
| **ROOM 2047**<br>PRESENTATIONS<br>Chair:<br>*Dawn Bennett (AUS)* | **ROOM 2048**<br>PRESENTATIONS<br>Chair:<br>*Sheila C. Woodward (ZAF)* | **ROOM 2049**<br>WORKSHOP<br>Chair:<br>*Hanne Orrenmaa (FIN)* | |
| [Practice Paper] *Anette Hamelink, Adrie Gloudemans (NLD)*<br>Incredibox and Spoken Word: The Combination of Dutch Language Lessons, Music Lessons and Digital Media in Primary Schools in Arnhem, the Netherlands | [Practice Paper] *Suyun Tang (SGP)*<br>An Inter-Art Approach to Develop a Seeing Ear and Hearing Eye | [Workshop] *Gerhard Lock, Marit Mõistlik-Tamm (EST)*<br>'All Together Now!': Five Inspiring Steps Towards Adventurous Musical Co-Creation | 11:30 |
| [Practice Paper] *Kateryna Zavalko (UKR)*<br>„Music-Children" Project: Mastering Playing in a Chamber Orchestra by Primary School Children | [Practice Paper] *Katharina Anzengruber (AUT)*<br>"KLANGKÖRPER – KÖRPER-KLANG". Experimenting with Sounds: An Interdisciplinary Approach to Teaching Arts and Natural Sciences | | 12:00 |

Practice Paper | Research Paper | Workshop

# THURSDAY, APRIL 20 | 14:00 – 20:30

| | PARALLEL-SESSIONS | | |
|---|---|---|---|
| | **ROOM "Bösendorfersaal"**<br>**PRiME Special Focus Group**<br>PRESENTATIONS<br>Chair:<br>*Wilfried Aigner (AUT)* | **ROOM "Hörsaal"**<br>PRESENTATIONS<br>Chair:<br>*Lee Higgins (GBR)* | **ROOM 2046**<br>PRESENTATIONS<br>Chair:<br>*Sarah Hennessy (GBR)* |
| 14:00 | *Michael Ahlers, Jule Landmeier (GER)*<br>Networking inside Communities Practicing Competence-Based Music Teaching | *Wolfgang Mastnak (GER)*<br>The Wealth of Mental Diversity: Psychopathological Challenges of Music in Schools | *Lina Oravec, Julia Lutz (GER)*<br>Learning from and with each Other – Embedding Cooperation of In-Service Generalist and Pre-Service Specialist Music Teachers in University Music Teacher Training |
| 14:30 | *Fabian Rieser (AUT/GER)*<br>Attachment Theory as a Tool to Enhance Teacher Reflexivity | *Dora Psaltopoulou-Kamini, Evangelia Chatziioannidou (GRE)*<br>Fundamental Training in Music Therapy Encourages Significant Changes in Music Students | *Sunny Choi (USA)*<br>Components Contributing to Development in the Field of Improvisation: Artistic Piano Interpretation of *Lean On* |
| 15:00 | *Roberto Cremades, Carlos Lage (ESP)*<br>Music and Images: Transversal-Participatory Approach for Music Creation in a Spanish Secondary Education Context | *Shirley Day-Salmon (AUT)*<br>Inclusive Music Making | *Vanessa Bond (USA)*<br>They Inspire Each Other: The Use of Music in a Reggio Emilia-Inspired School |
| 15:30 | COFFEE BREAK & POSTERTALK | | |
| | **ROOM "Bösendorfersaal"**<br>**PRiME Special Focus Group**<br>PRESENTATIONS<br>Chair:<br>*Isolde Malmberg (GER)* | **ROOM "Hörsaal"**<br>PRESENTATIONS<br>Chair:<br>*Shirley Salmon (AUT)* | **ROOM 2046**<br>**DOCTORAL STUDENT FORUM**<br>Chairs:<br>*Mary Stakelum (GBR)*<br>*Thade Buchborn (GER)* |
| 16:00 | *Wilfried Aigner (AUT)*<br>Encouraging Students to Compose in the Music Classroom and Social Web | *Jason Silveira, Jacob Close (USA)*<br>Music Education in Transition: Providing Support for Transgender Music Students | **Helbling-Session:**<br>*Markus Detterbeck (GER)*<br>From Action to Knowledge. Music Teaching: Creative and Logically Structured |
| 16:30 | *Motje Wolf, Sarah Younie (GBR)*<br>Enabling Access: Translating Music Education Research for Practitioners | *Stacey Garrepy (USA)*<br>'Musicking Together': A Practical Theory of Change for Music and Special Education | **DOCTORAL STUDENT FORUM (DSF)**<br>**Poster Presentation** |
| 17:00 | *Ute Konrad, Andreas Lehmann-Wermser (GER)*<br>Linking Theory Building to Classroom Intervention. A DBR-Study on Construction of Meaning | *Angelika Holzer (AUT)*<br>Dance ALL together! Students and Children with Special Needs Dance Together | |

17:45 – 18:45 **GENERAL MEETING | ROOM: "Kleines Studio"**

19:30 – 20:30 **"A Young Persons' Guide to Music Composed in Salzburg"** – Concert of Students of Salzburg Pre-College
**ROOM: "Solitär"**

| PARALLEL-SESSIONS | | | |
|---|---|---|---|
| **ROOM 2047**<br>**NC-SYMPOSIUM**<br>Chairs:<br>*Natassa Economidou Stavrou (CYP)*<br>*Andreas Bernhofer (AUT)* | **ROOM 2048**<br>PRESENTATIONS<br><br>Chair:<br>*Erik Esterbauer (AUT)* | **ROOM 2049**<br>WORKSHOP<br><br>Chair:<br>*Fritz Höfer (AUT)* | |
| **NATIONAL COORDINATORS' SYMPOSIUM**<br><br>**Joint Musical (Ad)ventures in Europe: Looking for Partners for Comparative Research and Practice Projects** | *Ilonka Pucihar (SLO)*<br>Music and Movement: An Indivisible Whole | **Yamaha-Workshop:**<br>*Sven Stagge (GER)*<br>Keyboard*Class* | 14:00 |
| | *Maria Papathanasiou (GBR/GRC)*<br>Music and Literature in Connection with Society: An Educational, Sociological and Humanistic Approach | | 14:30 |
| | *Paulo Esteireiro, Carlos Gonçalves (PRT)*<br>The Development of an Artistic Education Network with Students from Extracurricular Activities: Ten Years of the Project Artistic Season (2006–2016) | | 15:00 |
| COFFEE BREAK & POSTERTALK | | | 15:30 |
| **ROOM 2047**<br>PRESENTATIONS<br><br>Chair:<br>*Thomas De Baets (BEL)* | **ROOM 2048**<br>**SYMPOSIUM**<br><br>Chair:<br>*Adri de Vugt (NLD)* | **ROOM 2049**<br>WORKSHOPS<br><br>Chair:<br>*Marina Gall (GBR)* | |
| *Warren Haston (USA)*<br>A Joint Extracurricular Musical Venture between an Elementary School and a Private University | *Christopher Wallbaum, Christian Rolle, Daniel Prantl, Simon Stich, Joshihisa Matthias Kinoshita (GER), Sarah Hennessy (GBR), Olle Zandén (SWE)*<br><br>**Comparing Music Lessons: The Application of Different Guiding Ideas** | *Panagiota Papageorgiou (GRC)*<br>Connecting Music with the Study of People and Cultures through Active Experiences with World Music: The Example of a Maori Stick Game-Song | 16:00 |
| *Eva Koeniger (AUT)*<br>Klasse musizieren! Insights into the Project "ELEMU" in Viennese Primary Schools | | *Fritz Höfer (AUT)*<br>Computer and Tablet Support in 'Classroom Music' | 16:45 |
| *Athina Fytika, Elesa Papakosta-Smyri (GRC)*<br>Drawing Compositions: Introducing Contemporary Art to Kindergarten-Children through Piano-Experimentation | | | |

Practice Paper | Research Paper | Workshop

# FRIDAY, APRIL 21 | 8:40 – 14:00

08:40 **POSTER-SESSION: all Posters in short Flashlightpresentations**
Chair: Gerhard Sammer (GER) | ROOM "Solitär"

09:00 **KEYNOTE: David Irving (AUS)**
**Looking beneath Exoticism: Cultural Hybridity and Connected Histories in Early Modern European Music**
Chair: Michaela Schwarzbauer (AUT) | ROOM: "Solitär"

10:00 **BREAK**

| | PARALLEL-SESSIONS | | |
|---|---|---|---|
| | **ROOM "Bösendorfersaal"** PRESENTATIONS Chair: *Rûta Kanteruka (LVA)* | **ROOM "Hörsaal"** PRESENTATIONS Chair: *Sheila C. Woodward (ZAF)* | **ROOM 2046** PRESENTATIONS Chair: *Lorraine O'Connell (IRL)* |
| 10:15 | *Helmut Schaumberger (AUT)* The Professional Director of Children's Choirs and Youth Choirs: Findings of a Study on Special Training Courses in Austria | *Susan O'Neill, Yaroslav Senyshyn (CAN)* Enhancing Learners' Engagement in Collaborative Practices in the Music Classroom through a Focus on Reciprocity | *Anna Maria Kalcher (AUT)* "Schmiede Hallein": An Interdisciplinary Cultural Project as Inspiration and Model for Music Education |
| 10:45 | *Patrick Freer (USA)* The Singing of Adolescent Boys: Recent Research and a New Conceptualization of Instruction | *Emiel Heijnen, Melissa Bremmer (NLD)* Performances, Social Interventions & Transformations: Interdisciplinary Arts Educational Design | *Pinar Besevli Solmaz, Gülin Öziskender (TUR)* An Assessment of the "Black Sea Meets Vienna" Project |
| 11:15 | COFFEE BREAK | | |
| | **ROOM "Bösendorfersaal"** PRESENTATIONS Chair: *Helmut Schaumberger (AUT)* | **ROOM "Hörsaal"** PRESENTATIONS Chair: *Thomas De Baets (BEL)* | **ROOM 2046** PRESENTATIONS Chair: *Franz Niermann (AUT)* |
| 11:30 | **Helbling-Workshop:** *Markus Detterbeck (GER)* Pop Choral Singing in School- and Youth-Choirs | *Vicky Charisi (GBR)* Social Interactions in Computer-Supported Collaborative Music-Making in Early Childhood | *Akosua Addo (USA), Yiannis Miralis (CYP)* Transnational Dialogues in World Music Pedagogy: Interactions across Continents |
| 12:00 | | *Valerie Krupp-Schleußner (GER)* Social Justice and the Capability Approach: Theoretical and Empirical Accounts in the Context of Music Education | *Maura Thornton, Kate Heneghan (IRL)* "Westport-Scoil-Cheoil": An (Ad)Venture that Explores Multiple Facets of Transmission in Irish-Traditional-Music |

12:30 **LUNCH**

**DANCE PERFORMANCE (12:45 & 13:15): danceLABmusgym (Musisches Gymnasium Salzburg)**
**ROOM: "Kleines Studio"**

| PARALLEL-SESSIONS | | | |
|---|---|---|---|
| **ROOM 2047**<br>PRESENTATIONS<br>Chair:<br>*Martin Losert (AUT)* | **ROOM "Kleines Studio"**<br>**PANEL DISCUSSION**<br>Chair:<br>*Michaela Schwarzbauer (AUT)* | **ROOM 2049**<br>WORKSHOP<br>Chair:<br>*Lina van Dooren (SWE)* | |
| *Ciaran Deloughry (IRL)*<br>Who Pays and Who Plays? Mapping the Discourse of Publicly Funded Instrumental Music Education in Ireland | *Georg Steinschaden,*<br>*Ludwig Nussbichler (AUT)*<br><br>**Pre-College:**<br>**A Joint Adventure?** | *Anita Gritsch (AUT)*<br>Body Music | 10:15 |
| *Arkadiusz Bialak (SGP)*<br>Learning Elementary Harmony and Keyboard Skills through a Collaborative Approach | | | 10:45 |
| COFFEE BREAK | | | 11:15 |
| **ROOM 2047**<br>PRESENTATIONS<br><br>Chair:<br>*Martin Losert (AUT)* | **ROOM "Solitär"**<br>**STUDENT FORUM**<br>Chairs:<br>*Branka Rotar Pance (SLO)*<br>*Oliver Krämer (GER)* | **ROOM 2049**<br>WORKSHOP<br><br>Chair:<br>*Elisabeth Wieland (AUT)* | |
| *Cristina Marin (AUT)*<br>Learning a Musical Instrument at School: Frameworks of Cooperation Between Music Schools and Regular Schools in Styria | **STUDENT FORUM**<br>**Workshop** | *Johannes Steiner (AUT)*<br>A Cappella Grooving: A New Way of Singing Pop Songs in Class | 11:30 |
| *Hans van Regenmortel (BEL)*<br>"UKELILA": An Artistic Catalyst for Musical Adventures in and outside Schools | | | 12:00 |

Practice Paper | Research Paper | Workshop

# FRIDAY, APRIL 21 | 14:00 – 17:15

| | PARALLEL-SESSIONS | | |
|---|---|---|---|
| | **ROOM "Bösendorfersaal"**<br>PRESENTATIONS<br>Chair:<br>*Bernhard Gritsch (AUT)* | **ROOM "Hörsaal"**<br>**DigiTiME Special Focus Group**<br>PRESENTATIONS<br>Chair:<br>*Fritz Höfer (AUT)* | **ROOM 2046**<br>PRESENTATIONS<br>Chair:<br>*Rûta Kanteruka (LVA)* |
| 14:00 | *Vaike Kiik-Salupere, Marylin Tilga (EST)*<br>What Singing Students Expect from their Studio Teacher During One-to-One Singing Lessons and how to Improve the Formal Music Teachers' Education | *Marina Gall, Doug Bott, Jonathan Westrup (GBR)*<br>The Use of Technologies to Support the Musical Development of Young People with Special Educational Needs/Disabilities ("SEN/D") | *Natassa Economidou-Stavrou (CYP)*<br>Hitting a Tube: Music Synergies amongst University and High School Students |
| 14:30 | *Teryl Dobbs, Elizabeth Hagedorn (USA)*<br>Cultural Relevance and the Singing Voice: An Ad/Venture in Re/Imagining Music Learning and Teaching | *Hubert Gruber, Josef Buchner (AUT)*<br>How to Create Inverted Classroom Videos for Teaching and Learning Music in and out of the Classroom | *Antonella Coppi (ITA)*<br>"Il Sistema": The Manifestation of an El Sistema Inspired Programme in Italy: An Investigation into the Pedagogical Goals and Challenges of Italian Music Education |
| 15:00 | *David Johnson (SWE)*<br>Playlist: A Critical Survey of Song Repertoire in Swedish Compulsory Schools | *Milena Petrovic (SRB)*<br>Integrating Multimedia Approaches into Music Performance with Music Education Students | *Vedrana Markovic (UKR)*<br>Initial Solfeggio Teaching with Visually Impaired Students in Montenegro: Examples of Openness and Cooperation with the "Resource Centre for Children and Youth in Podgorica" |
| 15:30 | COFFEE BREAK & POSTERTALK | | |
| | **ROOM "Bösendorfersaal"**<br>PRESENTATIONS<br>Chair:<br>*Helmut Schaumberger (AUT)* | **ROOM "Hörsaal"**<br>**DigiTiME Special Focus Group**<br>PRESENTATIONS<br>Chair:<br>*Marina Gall (GBR)* | **ROOM 2046**<br>PRESENTATIONS<br>Chair:<br>*Katharina Anzengruber (AUT)* |
| 16:00 | *Johannes van der Sandt (ITA)*<br>'Oh Boy!' Boys' Choirs: Do They Still Matter? | *Michele Biasutti, Eleonora Concina, Sara Frate (ITA)*<br>Assessing a Virtual Training Programme for In-Service Music Teachers | *Ertem Nalbantoglu (CYP), Sharon Lierse (AUS)*<br>Music Education in the Northern Part of Cyprus and Australia: A Joint (Ad)venture in Music |
| 16:30 | *Gabriel Imthurn (CHE)*<br>"Basis Check Voice": A Diagnosis Tool | *Mercedes Castillo-Ferreira, Manuel Ángel Puentes-Zamora (ESP)*<br>Sound-Art-Installation at Infant School: Space Music | *Anette Ziegenmeyer (GER)*<br>"KulturCampus Wuppertal" (KCW): An Interdisciplinary Project by Annette Ziegenmeyer and Björn Krüger |

17:00 – 17:15 **BREAK**

| PARALLEL-SESSIONS | | | |
|---|---|---|---|
| **ROOM 2047**<br>PRESENTATIONS<br><br>Chair:<br>*Anna Houmann (SWE)* | **ROOM 2048**<br>PRESENTATIONS<br><br>Chair:<br>*Franz Niermann (AUT)* | **ROOM 2049**<br>WORKSHOPS<br><br>Chair:<br>*Anna Maria Kalcher (AUT)* | |
| *Irena Müller-Brozovic (CHE)*<br>'Lost and Found'. The Focus on Music in Concerts within a Mediating Context:<br>The Theoretical Framework of a Planned Case Study | *Gwen Moore (IRL)*<br>"Musical Futures" in Ireland: Findings from a Pilot Study | *Rosa de las Heras Fernández (ESP)*<br>Introduction to Flamenco in a Primary Classroom | 14:00 |
| *Andreas Bernhofer, Monika Oebelsberger, Petra Brüderl (AUT)*<br>Joint Venture:<br>University – School – Festival | *Judita Kučerová (CZE)*<br>Folk Song in Czech Schools: A Challenge for Music Education and Ethnomusicology? | *Johannes Treß (GER)*<br>"(How) Can I Learn to Improvise?": A Multidimensional Approach to Improvisation in Practice | 14:45 |
| *Katharina Schilling-Sandvoß, Anselma Lanzendörfer (GER)*<br>Discovering Music: A Cooperative Project between Music University, Schools and Concert Hall | *Albert Casals, Cristina González-Martín, Carmen Carrillo (ESP)*<br>"Impactmus": Analyzing the Impact of Music Education in Spain | | |
| COFFEE BREAK & POSTERTALK | | | 15:30 |
| **ROOM 2047**<br>PRESENTATIONS<br><br>Chair:<br>*Bernhard Gritsch (AUT)* | **ROOM 2048**<br>PRESENTATIONS<br><br>Chair:<br>*Monika Oebelsberger (AUT)* | **ROOM 2049**<br>WORKSHOP<br><br>Chair:<br>*Elisabeth Wieland (AUT)* | |
| *Irena Müller-Brozovic (CHE)*<br>Different Perspectives of People Involved in a Participative Project. Report and Reflection on a Project Realized by a 5th-Grade Class, the Basel Symphony Orchestra and Media Artists | *Teryl Dobbs (USA)*<br>"Performing the Jewish Archive" and its Potential for Joint (Ad)Ventures in Music Education | *Psyrra Vasiliki (GER)*<br>Music Begins Where Words End | 16:00 |
| *Claudia Cerachowitz (GER)*<br>Oskar and his Friends: Initiating and Organizing the Development of Music and Arts in School | *John Kratus (USA)*<br>Martin Buber in the Music Classroom | | 16:30 |

Practice Paper | Research Paper | Workshop

# FRIDAY, APRIL 21 | 17:15 – 22:00

| | PARALLEL-SESSIONS | | |
|---|---|---|---|
| | **ROOM "Bösendorfersaal"**<br>PRESENTATIONS<br>Chair:<br>*Gerhard Sammer (GER)* | **ROOM "Hörsaal"**<br>**DigiTiME Special Focus Group**<br>PRESENTATIONS<br>Chair:<br>*Wilfried Aigner (AUT)* | **ROOM 2046**<br>PRESENTATIONS<br>Chair:<br>*Lorraine O'Connell (IRL)* |
| 17:15 | *Johannes van der Sandt (ITA)*<br>Community Singing: A Pathway to Social Capital – a Cross-Cultural Comparative Assessment of the Benefits of Singing Communities in South Tyrol and South Africa | *Desiree Garcia-Gil, Roberto Cremades, Elena Esteban-Muñoz (ESP)*<br>Flipped Classroom Methodology in the Music Lessons of Superior Education | *Rûta Girdzijauskiene, Emilija Sakadolskiene, Sandra Rimkutė-Jankuvienė (LTU)*<br>Network for Music Education: Lithuanian Case Study |
| 17:45 | *Maria Honsig (AUT), Maria Majno (ITA)*<br>European Mozart Ways | *Rûta Kanteruka (LVA)*<br>Teaching Music in the Differentiated Classroom | *Zhang Wenzhuo (USA)*<br>Integrated Multicultural Music Education: Pedagogies and Practices Using Chinese Music as a Model |

18:15 **OPEN SESSION of existing Special Focus Groups (DigiTiME, PRiME) and Open Space for New Ideas**
Meeting point: ROOM "Bösendorfersaal"

20:00 **CONFERENCE DINNER with Traditional Austrian Music by "Moz-Partie"**
Restaurant "Stieglkeller", Festungsgasse 10

| PARALLEL-SESSIONS | | | |
|---|---|---|---|
| **ROOM 2047**<br>PRESENTATIONS<br><br>Chair:<br>*Branka Rotar Pance (SLO)* | **ROOM 2048**<br>PRESENTATIONS<br><br>Chair:<br>*Marinus M. Verkuil (NLD)* | **ROOM 2049**<br>WORKSHOP<br><br>Chair:<br>*Erik Esterbauer (AUT)* | |
| *Tobias Emanuel Mayer (GER)*<br>The Bernstein-Effect: Stars of Classical Music as 'Infectious' Classroom Music Educators | *Vanessa Bond (USA)*<br>Culturally Responsive Education in Music Education Literature | *Peter Mall, Ralf-Olivier Schwarz (GER)*<br>School, Outreach and Community: Perspectives on Cross-Institutional Music Education | 17:15 |
| *Bernhard Gritsch, Magdalena Steinmayr (AUT)*<br>"B9 – Beethoven for All" | *Jereon Vanesser (BEL)*<br>Music Teacher or Music Educator | | 17:45 |

Practice Paper | Research Paper | Workshop

# SATURDAY, APRIL 22 | 8:45 – 13:00

08:45 **Morning (AD)VENTURE: ROOM "Solitär"**

09:00 **KEYNOTE: Andreas Lehmann-Wermser (GER)**
**Why Some Joint Ventures Are Adventurous**
Chair: Andreas Bernhofer (AUT) | ROOM: "Solitär"

10:00 **Joint (AD)VENTURE MUSIC: Keynotespeakers' Reflection on the Congress**
Chair: Gerhard Sammer (GER) | ROOM: "Solitär"

10:15 **BREAK**

| | PARALLEL-SESSIONS | | |
|---|---|---|---|
| | **ROOM "Bösendorfersaal"**<br>PRESENTATIONS<br>Chair:<br>*Carola Schormann (GER)* | **ROOM "Hörsaal"**<br>PRESENTATIONS<br>Chair:<br>*Anna Maria Kalcher (AUT)* | **ROOM 2046**<br>**SYMPOSIUM**<br>Chair:<br>*Franz Niermann (AUT)* |
| 10:30 | *Erik Esterbauer (AUT)*<br>Assessment of the Quality of Relationship in Music Lessons: A New Approach | *Zsuzsanna Hegedűsné Tóth (HUN)*<br>"Music in Everything": A Novel Approach in Teaching Music to Young Children Using their Creativity | *Irena Medňanská (SVK), Miloš Kodejška, Marek Sedláček, Renata Horáková (CZE), Noemi Maczelka (HUN), Gabriela Konkol, Miroslav Dymon (POL)*<br>The Establishment of New Scientific Disciplines in the Systematics of Music Pedagogy: The Integration of Ideas Derived from Musicology, Pedagogy as Science and Other Social Disciplines and Art<br><br>How Do Young People Accept Contemporary Art Music? A Research into Musical Attitudes of University Students in the Czech Republic<br><br>Adventures within Music: International Youth Projects in the Music Education Department of Szeged University<br><br>Music and Arts Education at Youth Culture Centers in Poland |
| 11:00 | *Persefoni Tzanaki (GBR)*<br>The Impact of Empathy on Social Rhythmic Entrainment in Children's Musical Interaction: Cognitive and Motor-Emotional Approaches | *Gabriele Schellberg (GER)*<br>How Musical Do Primary Generalist Student Teachers Consider Themselves? | |
| 11:30 | *Sezgin Inceel (GER)*<br>'We Get Happy – We Write a Song. We Have a Funeral – We Lament.' Turkish Immigrant Parents' Educational Beliefs and Practices | *Giovanna Carugno (ITA)*<br>Scarlatti and his Harpsichord: A Mixed Pedagogical Approach to Teaching Music History at Primary School Level | |

**12:15 – 13:00** **CLOSING CEREMONY**
ROOM "Solitär"

**Closing Speeches and Thank You Note**
EAS President
Monika Oebelsberger (Mozarteum University Salzburg)
**Presentation of EAS 2018 in Jelgava/Riga (Latvia):**
Rûta Kanteruka (Chair of Organizing Committee)

**Music**
**The BBB "Pluskurs Big Band" (Privatgymnasium Borromäum Salzburg)**

| PARALLEL-SESSIONS | | | |
|---|---|---|---|
| **ROOM 2047**<br>PRESENTATIONS<br>Chair:<br>*Helmut Schaumberger (AUT)* | **ROOM 2048**<br>**SYMPOSIUM**<br>Chair:<br>*Michael Pabst-Krüger (GER)* | **ROOM 2049**<br>WORKSHOP<br>Chair:<br>*Rûta Girdzijauskiene (LTU)* | |
| *Rainer Brinkmann, Anne-Kathrin Ostrop (GER), Monika Oebelsberger (AUT)*<br>Joint (Ad)venture Opera | **PLATFORM FOR MUSIC TEACHER ASSOCIATIONS (MTA) IN EUROPE** | *Sonja Stibi (AUT)*<br>From Canon to Creation | 10:30 |
| *Rhoda Dullea (IRL)*<br>Creative Teaching Enabling Engagement with Opera in a Summer Camp Program for Adolescents | | | 11:30 |

Practice Paper | Research Paper | Workshop

# KEYNOTE SPEAKERS

**Susan O'Neill**

## Exploring a "Learning Lives" Approach to Connection and Collaboration in Music Education

©Dale Northey

In this talk, I explore a "learning lives" approach through two research projects conducted in Canada. These studies involved in-depth, individual interviews with nearly 100 young people aged 10 to18 years who were engaged in music learning in both school and outside school contexts. The term "learning lives" refers to the study of a range of social and educational contexts in which young people engage in music learning across physical and virtual life spaces and places at home, school, and within local and online communities. By examining learning across these different learning sites, we are able to gain a deeper understanding of learner identity across these different 'locations' and the multiple pathways through which young people make meaningful and purposeful connections with music. The aim of this work is to gain insights into the unique configurations of music learning ecologies that young people inhabit. In addition, this work helps us to highlight the usefulness of engaging students in documenting personal music learning environments. This also forms the basis for teacher-student and peer collaborative inquiry into the value of music in students' everyday lives. A focus on 'snapshots' of learning ecologies illustrates the potential of a learning lives approach for encouraging teachers' collaborative efforts to make music learning both relevant and engaging within current 21$^{st}$ century learning frameworks. For example, instead of viewing formal and informal music learning as two separate worlds, a learning lives approach makes it possible to find ways of understanding interconnections between different musical ecologies as experienced by young people. In doing so, we may begin to revision our research and educational practices in ways that align better with young people's socially engaged practices.

Susan O'Neill is Professor and Associate Dean, Academic and Research at Simon Fraser University and Director of MODAL Research Group (Multimodal Music Opportunities, Diversity and Learning). She is President-Elect of the International Society for Music Education and Senior Editor of the Canadian Music Educators' Association book series *Research to Practice*. She serves on the editorial boards of prominent music education and music psychology research journals, and has published widely in the fields of music psychology and music education, including chapter contributions to fifteen books published by Oxford University Press.

**David Irving**

## Looking beneath Exoticism: Cultural Hybridity and Connected Histories in Early Modern European Music

Multiculturalism and cultural sensitivity have for many decades been key issues in debates about music education. Specialists in ethnomusicology, gender and sexuality studies, popular music, and politics have questioned the values and ideologies implicit in the privileged status of Western art music. Increasingly, traditional core subjects such as literacy in staff notation or chronological music history are scrutinized critically within secondary and tertiary education, and some argue that they have no place in a culturally and socially inclusive curriculum. Reasons for this view include claims that Western art music is culturally exclusive and elite, and that this artform is aligned with the perpetuation of social inequality. Of course, Western art music is not innocent of the charge of cultural imperialism: for over five centuries it has been intertwined with the processes of global colonialism. Yet it is entirely misleading to assume and sustain some kind of conceptual, aesthetic, and educational dichotomy between Western art music and all other musics. Western art music is an inherently hybrid cultural practice, and the formation of the canon as we know it has been thoroughly dependent on exchanges and absorption of ideas from the rest of the world. Many musicologists have made extensive studies of European composers' (ad)ventures in musical exoticism, evoking other cultures, through music, text, and image. However, beneath these representations there are also 'hidden hybridities', including instruments, genres, aesthetics, and social structures. These were produced by processes of absorption and naturalization, through which the extra-European origins of certain influences were gradually, and usually passively, forgotten. Music in and from early modern Europe, c1500–c1800, was an artform that was in flux, subject to many outside influences and processes of internal change and renewal. While the cultural imperialism of the nineteenth and twentieth century projected and promoted the canon of Western art music as a kind of 'universal standard', early modern European music was still in dialogue with other cultures, and heavily indebted to them, although it was also used as a vehicle for colonialist agendas. Its history is thus a connected one, fully integrating Europe within the world. This lecture is a kind of polemical apologia for the presence of early modern European music in today's multicultural music curricula; it cites numerous examples of the active appropriation of European staff notation and performance practices by non-Europeans in the early modern period, and explores the role of the world in shaping an artform whose origins are not merely 'Western', but global. I argue that the teaching and practice of this music need not be seen by teachers or students as exclusionary or privileged, so long as it is fully contextualized, carefully interpreted, and sensitively framed.

David R. M. Irving is Senior Lecturer in Musicology at the Melbourne Conservatorium of Music, University of Melbourne. He researches the role of music in intercultural exchange, colonialism, and globalization. His publications include the monograph *Colonial Counterpoint: Music in Early Modern Manila* (Oxford University Press, 2010), numerous articles and book chapters, and the edited collection *Intercultural Exchange in Southeast Asia: History and Society in the Early Modern World* (I. B. Tauris, 2013), co-edited with early modern historian Tara Alberts (University of York). As a baroque violinist he has performed with many early music ensembles in Europe and Australia. He is the 2015 recipient of the McCredie Musicological Award from the Australian Academy of the Humanities, of which he has also been elected a Fellow.

**Andreas Lehmann-Wermser**

## Why Some Joint Ventures Are Adventurous

Joint ventures are usually met with great expectations as shared or complementary competencies and strengths are expected to lead to better performance, more joy or outstanding outcome. No wonder, joint actions are promoted in music education, too: Instrumental cooperate with general music teachers, orchestra musicians join school classes, composers in residence work with secondary school kids. However, those who cooperate oftentimes experience obstacles and working conditions that turn the welcomed ventures into unpredictable ADventures: organizing may be difficult, not all partners may be familiar with pedagogical skills needed to cope with school children and youths, planning needs more time and communication may be difficult. However, several studies have been conducted during the last years that shed some light on the questions involved and encourage us that it is possible to identify favorable conditions and give hints for successful collaborative teaching.

Dr. Andreas Lehmann-Wermser taught music in secondary schools for nearly two decades before he started his scientific career. He earned a degree as Dr. phil. from the Hannover University of Music Drama and Media in 2002. 2005 he was appointed associate professor at Bremen University where he founded a research group engaging in large empirical studies. His studies on cultural participation and competence models in music learning triggered several other studies and research projects. Since 2015 he is Director of the Institute for Music Education Research in Hannover. Besides numerous publications he is co-editor of the online journal *bulletin of empirical music education research* and has presented in a number of countries.

# ABSTRACTS

## RESEARCH PAPERS

**Akosua Addo (University of Minnesota) / Yiannis Miralis (European University Cyprus, Nicosia)**

### Transnational Dialogues in World Music Pedagogy: Interactions across Continents

This presentation focuses on a Collaborative Online International Learning (COIL) graduate course in music education at two institutions in Europe and the USA. Experiences and dialogues between music educators from the two countries provided opportunities for continuous professional development and for building professional networks within and across countries. The questions of this project were:

(1) How do transnational dialogues facilitate implementing world music in education?

(2) How do transnational dialogues provide teachers with supportive experiences and feedback while implementing world music content?

(3) To what extent do available academic technologies enrich the learning experiences of participants?

Through a detailed description of the course material and assignments we will examine how the enriched experiences of the participants enabled their involvement in world music pedagogy. Data was collected through focused interviews with participants who, simultaneously, served as culture bearers and novice learners of world music. Their dual identity was further investigated through an examination of their thoughts and reflections, as documented in their solicited journal narratives.

Students were asked to provide visual autobiographies, sharing musical identities in the form of digital stories, connecting with local immigrant communities and investigating musical case studies of immigrants. Graduate students reflected on and shared their musical culture and identity, communicated effectively across cultures and collaborated in small groups within and outside of class. These experiences resulted in a broadening of student understanding of world music and contribute towards music education and global social change. The experience was challenging both for students and instructors, and there were many implications for participants and education in general.

We share lessons learned from interactions with students, instructional designer, and faculty, and present the overall outcomes of an innovative educational project that can directly impact decision-making in world music education.

**Michael Ahlers / Jule Landmeier (Institute of Arts, Music and Mediation, Lueneburg)**

### Networking inside Communities Practicing Competence-Based Music Teaching

In April 2016, a new project arose at the Leuphana University of Lüneburg, Germany. Several professors and (post-) doctoral students gathered in order to permanently improve the quality of teacher training and education. Striving for a closer interconnection between theory and practice, as well as a better correspondence between universities and schools, a network of agents was – and is still being – established. Three categories form the basis of this project, namely: 'Heterogeneity and Inclusion', 'Profession-Based Support Systems' and 'Competence-Based Teaching'. Recognizing the importance and special challenges of music education, one entire branch of the competence-based teaching research is fully contributed to this subject.

Regarding the term 'competence', there are still some major issues to be addressed concerning its definition and use, which is especially noticeable when it comes to music. Additionally, there are hardly any materials available for music teachers willing to try out more competence-based approaches to music teaching. One of the main objectives for this project is therefore to examine existing materials, identifying whether or not they truly focus on competences, and based on that, creating and evaluating new materials inside a community of practice (CoP). In order to develop materials that effectively adapt to the everyday needs of schools, students and university staff work closely with experienced, open-minded music teachers. First outcomes of a specifically designed masters-level seminar reviewing and testing competence-based materials on problem-solving will be presented, as well as thoroughly discussed and reflected upon. While not a lot of empirically substantiated work on the efficiency, advantages and limitations of competence-based education in music has been done yet, we believe that striving for a more competence-based approach in music education could greatly benefit a student's learning experience as well as his/her long-term learning outcomes. Furthermore, the benefits of trans-disciplinary networks will be addressed.

Wilfried Aigner (University for Music and Performing Arts Vienna)

## Encouraging Students to Compose in the Music Classroom and Social Web

The presentation will summarize the results of a design-based research (DBR) study focused on the interrelations among creating music, the use of web-based technology and communication in a classroom context. The twin objectives of a DBR-study are to implement innovative solutions into teaching practice and to simultaneously generate theoretical understanding through iterative evaluation and reflection.

Current literature on the combination of composition and digital technology as activities in music classes internationally formed the theoretical basis of the study. The core data resulted from the empirical research on a two-year composition project, which brought together students in Austrian schools with a team of mentors (consisting of teachers, composers and student tutors) in workshops and lessons, in addition to also using online music notation and online mentoring as creation and communication systems. Students used "Noteflight", a web-based music notation tool, to create their own pieces of music, and the LMS "Moodle" as a tool to communicate online.

The results of the study take the form of design principles which yield context-related knowledge that can be applied to similar design settings. Most important aspects include

- the potential of online music notation and online communication for students composing music
- the dichotomy between instruction and independence in the context of music technology and the social web
- the interaction and roles of the people involved in a blended learning setting that focuses on musical creation
- the interplay of the online world and live music experience and its meaning for the compositional process.

Finally, the results permit perspectives on the future of web-technology-based composition in the music classroom.

Michele Biasutti / Eleonora Concina / Sara Frate (University of Padova)

## Assessing a Virtual Training Programme for In-Service Music Teachers

The current research intends to verify if in-service music teachers could benefit from an online educational experience focused on reflective skills improvement. A collaborative online course for professional development of in-service instrumental and vocal music teachers of the Trentino Music schools has been designed and the students' satisfaction has been assessed. The educational program has been developed considering the principles of collaborative learning during an academic year. A socio-constructivist perspective has been adopted to design a web-based educational context where teachers contributed to share knowledge in order to improve their professional skills and competences. The participants (N=22) were engaged in collaborative learning activities in online and face to face settings. Online lessons consisted of activities which included forum discussions and Wikis experiences, while during face to face activities workshops were offered. The didactic contents of the online training programme covered several dimensions of teaching pedagogy and music education, and were planned in order to fulfil the professional development needs of music teachers. At the end of the annual activities, participants had to discuss a project-work which was collaboratively designed in small groups in a Wiki virtual environment within the Moodle platform.

Data about participants' satisfaction were collected with a mixed method including quantitative and qualitative instruments. Quantitative data were analysed using statistical analysis (Biasutti, 2012) and qualitative data were subjected to an inductive content analysis of the final focus groups (Biasutti, & EL-Deghaidy, 2015). The analysis identified the aspects of the collaborative learning experience considered most important and the aspects that should be improved. In addition, results have shown the professional development that participants reported in their teaching activity. The key factors that contributed to the effectiveness of the course as well as implications for designing activities for the professional development of instrumental teachers are also discussed.

Vanessa Bond (University of Hartford's The Hartt School)

## Culturally Responsive Education in Music Education Literature

Demographic shifts in school enrollment within the United States and throughout Europe necessitate preparing pre-service teachers to teach students with backgrounds that differ from their own ethnically, linguistically, racially, and economically. Culturally responsive education (CRE) is a pedagogy used to validate students' varied experiences, and to teach to and through their strengths. CRE emphasizes high expectations, the formation of cultural competence, and development of a critical consciousness. Although the philosophical principles of culturally responsive education have been addressed in general education literature for over thirty years, the presence of CRE in music education dialogue is a relatively recent phenomenon. In this session, I will share a literature review with the purpose of describing how and for what purposes culturally responsive education has been addressed in the music education literature.

**Vanessa Bond (University of Hartford's The Hartt School)**

## They Inspire Each Other: The Use of Music in a Reggio Emilia-Inspired School

The Reggio Emilia approach (REA) is a prominent approach to early childhood education found around the globe. Heralded as one of the best schools in the world, the REA is based on the teaching principles and foundational philosophies of the infant-toddler centers and preschools in the municipality of Reggio Emilia, Italy. Although each Reggio-inspired adoption of the Italian schools vary by setting, any school claiming Reggio inspiration is grounded in social constructivism, an emergent curriculum, and learning through multiple modes of expression. Traditionally, the varied modes of expression have manifested in a fine arts focus with marker, paint, wire, and other artistic mediums serving as languages for children. Music, although mentioned as a mode of children's expression in the REA-related literature, is less documented.

The purpose of this case study was to investigate the use of music in one Reggio Emilia-inspired preschool in the United States. I spent over sixty hours across a three-week timeframe collecting field note and audio-recorded data at the study site. During this time I interacted with all children and staff of the school, noting all emergent experiences and teaching processes related to music. I interviewed all stakeholders (i.e., administrator, teachers, parents) to gather varied perspectives about the use of music at school and in the lives of children. I analyzed all written and recorded data, categorizing children's spontaneous musicking and using several cycles of coding to identify prominent themes. In this research presentation I will share highlights of the final report using a mixture of descriptive techniques, including vignettes, detailed narratives, interview transcript excerpts, reflective memos, audio recordings and direct quotation of children's dialogue as recorded during fieldwork.

**Thade Buchborn / Elisabeth Theisohn (Hochschule für Musik Freiburg)**

## "Was our Song Already Good?" Criteria-Based Processes of Composing Music in School

Even though nearly 90% of the German curricula for music in school contain tasks related to creativity (Hasselhorn, 2015), pupils as well as teachers often miss the tools or criteria to evaluate creative processes and products. Furthermore creativity and creative skills seem to be hard to describe in research-based competence models (Hasselhorn, 2015; Lehmann, 2005; Hickey, 2001).

In our design-based research study we initialise and design processes of group composition in the music classroom (Burnard, 2013) and develop criteria for creative tasks. A qualitative analysis of the discussions in the working groups gives us information about criteria that are helpful for children to compose and to evaluate their works and those of others.

By this research-based design of criteria for creative tasks, we hope to offer ways of learning composition in class that are based on transparent criteria and open up space for reflection and meta-cognition, which are key features of self-directed learning and a learner-centred music education.

Furthermore our research might give information for the development and validation of a competence model for generative performance (Lehmann, 2005and 2008), that is still missing in research and every day work in schools.

In our presentation we will show first results of our study as well as lesson examples and discuss our method in the context of other approaches to design research (Prediger et al., 2015).

**Seyhan Bulut (Music Conservatory / Music and Fine Arts Institute, Samsun)**

## The Function of Instrument-Masters' Video Lessons in Conservatory Education

Instrumental education is simply a master-apprentice model. Thus, at conservatories, instrumental courses are carried out one-to-one. The master provides the student with knowledge and experience to be able to play the instrument at an advanced level. In graduation, as a final test to prove the students' maturity on their instruments, the students play some chosen repertoire in order to demonstrate their mastery in instrumental technique, musicality, expression, stylistic interpretation and stage performance at an advanced level. Within this process, the masters whom the students work with throughout the education period at conservatory play a significant role.

In the past, conservatory students could work with only one master, except when another master visited their conservatory or a concert hall nearby, or when students travelled to meet other masters. Therefore, the opportunity to attend the live workshops and masterclasses of world-famous instrumentalists was a matter of fortune. Within the last century, students have gained more access to masters because of the increased prominence of the recording industry and internet. Within the first half of the 20th century, the new option was to purchase masters' recordings. However, recently, as internet is becoming more functional day by day, new options arouse for conservatory students, instrumentalists and teachers, enabling them to work with a professional online, one-to-one.

This paper aims to exemplify some of the recent online professional instrumental lessons from world-famous instrumentalists and to raise awareness on the functionality of these publications in instrument education at the conservatories. It is argued that video lessons are very useful multimedia publications and are getting established as a new section within instrumental education literature. Therefore it is suggested that masters should be encouraged to publish such multimedia so that conservatory libraries can provide access to these materials.

**Albert Casals / Cristina González-Martín (Universitat Autònoma de Barcelona) /**
**Carmen Carrillo (University of Catalonia)**

## "Impactmus": Analyzing the Impact of Music Education in Spain

Music education in Spain has been part of compulsory education since the early nineties. More than 20 years later, it is time to wonder about the impact of music education on new generations and to analyse, based on research evidence, the role that Music can play – if any – within the school system. With this purpose, "IMPACTMUS" (EDU2014-58066-P) – a research project funded by the Spanish government- deals with the goal to produce evidence-based knowledge to determine the impact that music education in compulsory education has had over the last decades in Spain. It expects to be developed during the 2015 to 2018 period and uses a mixed research method design that includes, in the first stage, literature review, observations of music classes, case studies and life-stories and, in the second stage, questionnaires.

This paper aims at providing an overview of the methodological design of the project. It also seeks to highlight some of the key ideas that the review of the literature on the topic of the project has revealed and that focuses on the following issues: (1) there is a lot of academic literature on music education advocacy but there are only a few pieces of evidence regarding the real impact of music education in students; (2) most of the Spanish and Catalan literature on music education is focused on its impact on other specific subjects rather than its influence over music awareness or over personal development in general.

It must be kept in mind that observations of music classes, life-stories and case studies are still in process. Even so, with the data we are collecting, we expect to document the role that music education can play so that both the education system and the students taught in this system face the challenges of a society that emphasizes the acquisition of knowledge.

**Vicky Charisi (UCL, London)**

## Social Interactions in Computer-Supported Collaborative Music-Making in Early Childhood

This paper presents the results of a long-term study, which focused on the social interactions between children during a music-making activity. Previous research on computer-supported collaborative learning has shown that a variety of verbal and non-verbal behaviours facilitate the process of learning. However, considering the communicative nature of

music, in the case of real time music composition and improvisation in early childhood, the on-going musical outcome may function as a means to allow additional forms of communication to emerge between the children.
Participants of this study included N=16 children (8 girls) aged 53 to 79 months (M=69, SD=7,39). They were asked to create musical pieces in pairs in weekly sessions over a period of maximum eight weeks. Each pair of children was video-recorded separately in the computer lab of the school. The children were provided with digital tools with graphical user interface. Graphical representations of sounds and musical patterns were semantically displayed. Data that are presented in this paper are based on 1192 minutes of video-recordings.
A micro-genetic data analysis was performed after the transcription of the data. According to this analytical approach the emerged behaviours are coded in an iterative process with the aim to depict the process of change and the development of the behaviours.
A first level of analysis revealed 12 behaviours of social interaction, which were grouped into seven themes. They included balanced and imbalanced collaboration, socio-affective behaviours and socially oriented musically induced behaviours, such as social singing and social body movement. Despite the individual differences, the data analysis revealed patterns of social interactions. Task-related collaboration based on verbal data appeared in .43% of the data while non-verbal behaviours appeared in .32%. Social body movement appeared only in .02% but a qualitative analysis of those instances revealed their relevance to cognitive processes such as planning. Social interactions increased over time.
Implications of this study include the use of technology in music education and interaction design for children.

**Fanny Chung (The Chinese University of Hong Kong)**

## Interdisciplinary Approaches for Music Learning in Hong Kong

The applications of integrated approaches between music and the other school subjects in kindergartens have become increasingly popular in Hong Kong. The Hong Kong Pre-primary curriculum guide (2006) suggested that the integrated approaches should be adopted in early childhood education in Hong Kong, in which a relaxing and pleasurable learning environment that promotes a balanced approach to the various areas (physical, intellectual, linguistic, social, emotional, aesthetic) should be provided.
This study brought together a class of kindergarten children (aged six), a kindergarten teacher, and a researcher in a kindergarten in Hong Kong. This study aims at exploring the effectiveness as well as the problems and challenges in adopting the integrated approach in music classes for children. The content of the music classes in this project was designed to enhance children's various competency and knowledge in music through the use of concepts and activities borrowed from the other disciplines. As such, the children learned musical concepts and gained musical experience through various innovative play-based activities, e.g. creative dance, poems, visual arts, physical activities, drama.
In this study, three 35-minute music lessons were observed and videotaped. The design of music lessons was drawn from the literature on early childhood music education, integrated approaches, the Hong Kong pre-primary curriculum guide, and the theory of multiple intelligences by Howard Gardner. Data was derived from interviews with the class teacher, principal, observation field notes, and feedback by the researcher.
The findings revealed that the kindergarten children in this study were enthusiastic about participating in the creative and innovative music activities that relate to other subject areas. Furthermore, it was found that the integrated approach adopted in the music lessons not only promote children's competency and interest in music, but also enrich children's learning in other disciplines.

**Antonella Coppi (Free University of Bolzano)**

## "Il Sistema" – the Manifestation of an El Sistema Inspired Programme in Italy: An Investigation into the Pedagogical Goals and Challenges of Italian Music Education

My study has investigated the Italian "Il Sistema" Programme, inspired by the Venezuelan music education model, El Sistema. In the last decade many projects inspired by the Venezuelan experience have been initiated in Europe. In 2010, thanks to the stimulus of Maestro Claudio Abbado, El Sistema was established in Italy and called "Il Sistema delle Orchestre e dei Cori Giovanili e Infantili In Italia (Onlus)". Currently there are more than 65 "Il Sistema" programmes nationally. This study investigated into and analysed the different models according to their similarities, differences

and their application of the El Sistema pedagogical goals within the context of formal, informal and non-formal Italian music education settings. This research is the first critical investigation into the primary pedagogical approaches of the Italian "Il Sistema" – it explores the current state of art and educational goals of the Italian models.
Both quantitative and qualitative methods were used in the collection of data. Action research was a valuable source of data collection as it enabled the researcher direct access to many of the programmes and their characteristics. Results identified challenges of cooperative projects between schools and other institutions, but with a positive undercurrent showing that pedagogical approaches follow the principles of music making being used for social change and building bridges in a multicultural setting. This research, officially recognised in June 2015 by "Federculture" and by the "Comitato Nazionale Orchestre e cori giovanili ed infantili in Italia", will serve as the onset of reflection and important discussions as to the use of music education in different contexts and settings.

**Roberto Cremades / Carlos Lage (Universidad Complutense de Madrid)**

## Music and Images: Transversal-Participatory Approach for Music Creation in a Spanish Secondary Education Context

Action research study (McNiff & Whitehead, 2002) arose from the aim of the transformation of my classroom (Burnard, Apelgren & Cabaroglu, 2015) through an axis comprised of the creation of music, the active participation of the students' research (research and didactic), and via a series of didactic projects focused on the creation of music in conjunction with other visual arts manifestations (cross-modal perception).
A cross-curricular approach (Fautley & Savage, 2011) developed as a guide to composition, a source of motivation and to encourage the consideration of the cross-cutting nature of the arts from the perspective of their ties, as a reflexive element in which different languages merge into one unique, artistic manifestation (Trías, 2014)
We have tried to analyse the learning-teaching processes in the creation of music, by focusing on learning, the students' motivation in the didactic projects carried out, and the analysis of the innovative methodological proposals based on creativities (Burnard, 2012). The study took place in three Spanish secondary schools throughout five cycles from 2008 to 2013 in the region of Madrid. A multidimensional collaboration was established with the Madrid Complutense University and two professional artists. Various data (observation; interviews; classroom diary; classroom assessments; questionnaires; video and audio recordings) were classified, analysed and triangulated (Saunders y Somekh, 2009).
The following conclusions can be drawn:

(1) Students have recognised the value of individual and collective creation.
(2) The students' role as musicians was meaningful.
(3) Four interconnected pedagogic directions were found: student experimentation, teacher guidance, group-based learning, student-based learning.
(4) Positive emotions manifested themselves from both a multidimensional and dual (teacher-student) perspective.
(5) The identification of the students with the created music significantly influenced the classroom motivation level.

A participatory creativity conceptual map is proposed as a paradigm on musical learning in schools. The focus on learning via collective creativity through music as a holistic process can be determined by: students' participation, motivation, positive emotions, class environment / well-being and group identity.

**Ciaran Deloughry (Cork ETB School of Music)**

## Who Pays and Who Plays? Mapping the Discourse of Publicly Funded Instrumental Music Education in Ireland

Publicly funded instrumental music education in Ireland presents as a fee-paying extra-curricular activity provided by a small number of Education and Training Boards (ETB) through specialist instrumental Music Services. While concepts of universal access and inclusion underpin the primary- and secondary-level education sector, such discourses have less currency in the area of instrumental music education. Although the public music provision is substantially part-funded through general taxation, common cultural assumptions appear to place the learning of musical instruments within the educational choices of middle- and upper middle-class families to the exclusion of other social groups.
The paper explores 'taken-for-granted' belief systems of practitioners and organizations as factors which may be complicit in the reproduction of advantage. A series of interviews sought the perceptions of instrumental music education practitioners (N=14) in seven publicly-funded Music Services in Ireland. Findings show that within the Music Services,

aesthetic and pedagogic discourses of the 19th century Conservatory system exert a hegemonic influence over policy and practice. An enduring 'examination culture' located within the Western art music tradition determines pedagogy, musical genre, and assessment procedures. Ideologies of musical taste reinforce boundaries of fee-payment and restricted availability as a form of 'concealed selectivity'. The effective 'rationing' of publicly provided instrumental music tuition as a high-status out-of-school leisure activity affirms cultural differentials between social classes.
Study participants advocated the primary school as a socially equitable point of access to instrumental music education. However, practitioners expressed a common awareness of a status duality whereby visiting instrumental specialists in primary schools experience conflict between specialist and generalist educational aims. The study suggests a basis for rethinking instrumental music in the Irish education system as a reconciled specialist-generalist model of in-school musical participation.

**Teryl Dobbs (University of Wisconsin-Madison)**

## "Performing the Jewish Archive" and its Potential for Joint (Ad)Ventures in Music Education

"Performing the Jewish Archive", a global research project funded by the United Kingdom's AHRC (Large Grant), aims to create new means of conceptualizing music, theatre, and literature as archives in multiple contexts. By focusing on Jewish artists and their works (from c.1880 to the present) that were either hidden or suppressed due to oppression and displacement (particularly vis-à-vis the Holocaust), the project's overarching goal seeks to draw wider intercultural and ethical implications for society today, thus shaping arts policies and practices in the future. This is accomplished by mounting international performances and symposia of newly discovered works by Jewish musicians, dramatists, and authors, theorizing them as archives that reveal knowledge, values, emotions, ideologies, and beliefs of the eras and communities where they were created.
Fundamental to "Performing the Jewish Archive" is the intentional integration of joint (ad)ventures between public and private cultural institutions that, by employing culturally relevant pedagogy (Ladson-Billings, 2009/1994) and critical social reconstructionist perspectives (Apple, 2004; Sleeter & Grant, 2007) in music education settings, might assist young people to develop their musicking selves and provide multiple platforms where their authentic voices might be heard. Experiences such as these are key for active musical participation in rapidly changing societies, particularly for youth who identify with underrepresented minorities e.g. indigenous, immigrant, Roma, and African-American youth.
This paper employs the aforementioned theoretical frameworks to analyze primary source materials and multimedia data gathered from "Performing the Jewish Archive's" first 18 months. Central to the thesis is the re-discovery and narrative of pianist/composer Josima Feldschuh – suppressed and imprisoned within the Warsaw Ghetto during the Holocaust – and her creative work. Preliminary findings from the grant project suggest pedagogical implications for culturally relevant musicking experiences, particularly with minoritized young people, that have the potential to support all students' developing a deeper connection to their unique musical voices.

**Rhoda Dullea (University College Cork)**

## Creative Teaching Enabling Engagement with Opera in a Summer Camp Program for Adolescents

Summer camps are a mainstay of non-formal education for children and adolescents across North America and Europe, bridging the gap in formal education created by the summer vacation period. Such programmes offer a non-pressured learning environment where young people may immerse themselves briefly and intensively in a subject area and 'try out' new learning identities.
This qualitative case study examines the creative teaching approaches employed by a team of instructors working with adolescents in the Canadian Opera Company's Summer Opera Camp Senior Company in July 2016 at the home of COC in the Four Seasons Arts Centre, Toronto. Artist-educators from a number of operatic production domains (including performance, design and composition) joined forces to enable a creative encounter with opera through facilitation of a collaborative composition and performance project among young people with diverse artistic interests and competencies. Providing conceptual frameworks derived from contemporary and historical operatic practice, these educators worked together to generate a supportive environment for intensive, critically engaged creative activity among a small 'company' of young people of high-school age.

Methods used in the study included unstructured observation of rehearsal processes and semi-structured one-to-one interviews with educators, as well as a consideration of the material culture of the company's week-long production workshop. Results showed that the instructors engaged in reflexive teaching methods, adapting their approaches and their teaching plans to the individual needs of the participants and the collective needs of the group, supported the progress of the creative project at the camp. Participants demonstrated deep engagement in the collaborative creative project, and the majority expressed interest in participating in opera in the future, in undergraduate training and as audience members. The COC summer camp demonstrated the importance of non-formal 'taster' programmes by arts organisations for connecting young people with professional arts practice at a crucial age, when career choices are being consolidated.

**Erik Esterbauer (Mozarteum University Salzburg)**

## Assessment of the Quality of Relationship in Music Lessons: A New Approach

Teaching of music offers, thanks to the possibility to address cognitive, emotional, social and creative areas of the human being, an ideal basis for a holistic approach. Elementary Music & Dance Pedagogy (EMDP) can contribute especially to inclusive learning contexts through specific artistic-pedagogical interventions in heterogeneous groups. The fundamental effectiveness of pedagogical music and dance interventions is based on the distinction of the diverse abilities of children and the quality of relationship.

Due to the clear structure, applicability and high significance of the observation and evaluation instrument AQR (Assessment of the Quality of Relationship), the aim of this research project is an adaption of this music therapy tool for pedagogical use and in a second phase an investigation of the empirical impact of artistic-pedagogical interventions in music teaching.

The AQR-instrument consists of four scales which refer to different expression phenomena: the instrumental expression, the vocal-pre-speech quality, the physical-emotional expression and the therapist/pedagogue and his interventions. Each scale focuses on certain points of observation and is divided into seven relationship qualities ('modes'), described by qualitative and quantitative characteristics of relationship aspects. The assessment of the ability to relate with the help of the seven modes points to the respective capabilities and the current condition of the individual participants and thus provides important indications for the methodical approach and reflection of the therapist or teacher. Inclusive groups working in music and dance lessons (school and non-school context) have been videoed and selected scenes have been assessed with the existing AQR-instrument. Phenomena related to relationship matters not outlined in the AQR and relevant for pedagogical situations have been identified, classified and assessed. New aspects of observation criteria and modes of relationship quality have been generated and were validated through inter-rater reliabilities, leading to an expanded version of this instrument.

The AQR seems to be an appropriate tool for observing and assessing the quality of relationships in (inclusive) music education. Fundamental modifications and extensions of the AQR, to be discussed in my presentation, are necessary in order to apply this tool in the field of music education in school and non-school contexts.

**Daniel Fiedler / Daniel Müllensiefen (University of Education Freiburg)**

## Musical Trajectories and Creative Orientation of Music Lessons Affect the Development of Interest in 'Music' in Secondary School Students

Trajectories of musical development can be very different in the course of adolescence and the causes and mechanisms leading to these differences are often the focus of research in music education. To measure the aspects of musical development of German students, the psychometric constructs 'musical self-concept' and 'musical sophistication' can be used. The first aim of my repeated-measurement study was to identify different developmental trajectories within a sample of secondary school students. The second aim was to identify how 'musical self-concept' and 'musical sophistication' as well as a creative approach to music teaching (e.g. composing, improvising, drawing and dancing to music, etc.) contribute to the development of the target variable *interest in music as a school subject.*

Data of 167 students (f = 94, m = 73) from two grammar schools (n= 102) and two middle schools (n= 65) are presented. The data comprised the self-assessed psychometric constructs as well as music-specific and demographic background variables and the target variable of this study at four time points over a period of nearly two school years. The data were analyzed using sequence-pattern-analyses and multilevel models.

The sequence-pattern-analyses identified three developmental trajectories for the constructs 'musical self-concept' and 'musical sophistication'. In addition, significant associations between two typical identified developmental trajectories and the variables *sex (phi* = .299), *musical status (phi* = .221), and *self-assessed marks in 'music' (phi* = .242; only for the second measurement point) are found. A multilevel analysis shows that the two typical developmental trajectories affect students' *interest in 'music'* over the four time points. Additionally, the multilevel analysis shows that the *interest in 'music'* is decreasing ($p \leq .001$), but students in the high developmental trajectory demonstrate a significant higher interest in 'music' over time ($p \leq .001$), compared to their peers in the low trajectory group. Moreover, a further analysis shows that a creative approach to music teaching ($p \leq .05$) as well as the high developmental trajectory of students ($p \leq .001$) affect the development of *interest in 'music'*, while *interest in music as a school subject* is generally decreasing over time ($p \leq .001$).
Hence, this study makes an important contribution to the understanding of the mechanisms of musical development during adolescence.

**Patrick Freer (Georgia State University, Atlanta)**

## The Singing of Adolescent Boys: Recent Research and a New Conceptualization of Instruction

This presentation reports a review of recent research concerning the male adolescent voice change. Emphasis is placed on the pedagogical implications of that research, with attention to findings that confirm or are contrary to common instructional practice. The review was limited to research published in the past five years (2011–2016). A total of 816 published English-language articles were located using the terms 'adolescence', 'male', and 'voice change'. These were narrowed to 110 sources with application of the term 'singing' and/or the topic of vocal pedagogy. These sources were analyzed and sorted into categories. The results represent current scientific knowledge about the male changing voice, singing, motivation, and implications for pedagogy.
The anatomical process of male adolescent voice change has been well documented since the late 1970s (see Cooksey, 2000). The implications for concurrent vocal pedagogy are less clear, and many teachers either avoid differentiating instruction or are unsure of how to best meet the vocal and related psychological needs of these boys (Ashley, 2013; Freer, 2009; Harrison & Welch, 2012). Studies about boys and singing suggest that boys understand neither the physiological process of voice change nor the phonational and musical effects of the changes (Ashley, 2008/2009; Freer, 2009). A host of recent and related studies collectively indicates that adolescent boys' motivation for continued singing activity results from their self-perceptions of musical autonomy and vocal skill (Harrison, 2010; Sweet, 2010; Elorriaga, 2011; Abrahams, 2012; Collins, 2012; Freer, 2012; Legg, 2012; Bennetts, 2013).
This presentation concludes with specific pedagogical techniques drawn from the findings of the review. Practical exercises focus on the teaching of vocal skills to adolescent boys in both individual (studio) and group (rehearsal) settings. Exercises address the topics of breath control, vocalization, pitch matching, and range extension.

**Marina Gall (University of Bristol) / Doug Bott (OpenUp Music) / Jonathan Westrup (Drake Music)**

## The Use of Technologies to Support the Musical Development of Young People with Special Educational Needs/Disabilities ("SEN/D")

The founding of British Paraorchestra – the world's first professional ensemble of disabled musicians – in 2011, and particularly their world debut at the Paralympic Closing Ceremony in 2012, has been significant in establishing a new movement whose aim is "to recognise and showcase disabled musicians with extraordinary abilities" (The British Paraorchestra, 2013). This parallels innovative developments by a number of UK music educationists, working in educational settings ("Drake Music", undated; "Drake Music Scotland", undated; "OpenUp Music", 2016a).
I am a teacher educator who currently works with two charities – "OpenUp Music" (2016a) and "Drake Music" (undated) – that aim to support students and young people with special needs/disabilities (SEN/D) to make music, particularly through the use of innovative technologies.
This paper, will report on studies – also discussed in the latest EAS book *European Perspectives on Music Education: Creativity and Innovation* – that illustrate how new technologies, together with sound pedagogical approaches, are offering exciting new opportunities for young people who, hitherto, have not been able to participate, actively, in music-making.

The paper will include:

(1) student perceptions on workshops led by "Drake Music" that have been included in the one-year Music Initial Teacher Education (training) course that I lead in England (collected by questionnaire and interview);
(2) reflections on a recent research project in which I researched the work of "OpenUp Music" in one SEN/D secondary school in England. (Methods included videoing classroom music sessions, and also staff and parents discussions/interviews.)

We will explain key findings, including the potential of certain music technologies not only for use by young people with special needs/disabilities (SEN/D) but also within mainstream school music classes. Findings also suggest that this is a vital area for consideration by trainee music teachers.

**Desiree Garcia-Gil / Roberto Cremades (Universidad Complutense de Madrid) / Elena Esteban-Muñoz (Music at Universidad Autónoma de Madrid)**

## Flipped Classroom Methodology in the Music Lessons of Superior Education

The 'flipped classroom' means a change in the planning of traditional teaching. If, habitually, the explanation of the theoretical contents on the part of the teacher takes up a large amount of class time, in this pedagogic model, the transmission of information is made outside the classroom using audio-visual materials available in virtual platforms. Consequently, during the face-to-face lesson plan, it is possible to go into depth with the practical activities which consolidate the theoretical contents. The above mentioned planning of the educational strategies is especially relevant in the education of musical teaching where the procedural contents for the practical nature of the matter are more significant than the conceptual ones.
The present research studies the use of the flipped classroom in one of the music subjects within the official curriculum of the Bachelor's Degree in Early Childhood Education. This way, the theoretical contents of the study plan appear consecutively across a set of videos available in a virtual environment designed for the subject with an approximate duration of between five and ten minutes. The audio-visual material is provided five days before every session, so the group has enough time to access the content and to introduce the principal ideas that are going to be developed in the sessions.
Thus, the following question arises: What kind of relation exists between the use of the flipped classroom methodology, increased motivation and the acquisition of theoretical contents in pupils? The narrative model is taken as a research approach and 33 statements of pedagogic experiences are analysed according to the holistic system of content.
The obtained conclusions suggest that the above mentioned innovation of face-to-face education modifies the passive role of the pupil substantially, it promotes the role of the teacher as a guide and it increases collaborative and autonomous learning.

**Sezgin Inceel (Hochschule für Musik und Theater München)**

## 'We Get Happy – We Write a Song. We Have a Funeral – We Lament.' Turkish Immigrant Parents' Educational Beliefs and Practices

Research indicates that parents play an essential role in their children's musical and language development (Clair, Jackson & Zweiback, 2012; Davidson, Howe, Moore & Sloboda, 1996; De Houwer, 1999; Mallett, 2000). Moreover, neuro-cognitive studies point to the similarities between music and language processing (Patel, 2003; Schön, Gordon & Besson, 2005). Based on the previous literature, the present study focuses on the Turkish immigrant parents' beliefs and practices regarding three crucial educational areas: music education, bilingual language acquisition and benefits of music education for bilingual language acquisition. Interviews, observations, and post-activity questionnaires are applied to generate qualitative data. Comparisons of the results from three categories indicate that the participants' positive beliefs are influenced by distal factors (cultural features, parents' own backgrounds, and socio-demographical characteristics). However, the lack of theoretical knowledge regarding the subjects seems to have a negative impact on these beliefs. If parents are not able to look upon the subjects discussed critically, parent-child practices seem to come short, or they face different difficulties. In the light of this information, recommendations for practice (policy makers, practitioners, parents) and for further research are discussed at the end of the study.

David Johnson (Malmö Academy of Music)

## Playlist: A Critical Survey of Song Repertoire in Swedish Compulsory Schools

The forces shaping repertoire selection in Swedish music education today come from many diverse sources inside and outside the classroom: from both students and teachers, central government directives, commercial interests, demographic shifts and current research in the development of the voice. Because singing can be seen as such a fundamental aspect of music training for young children, much is at stake. Researchers have expressed concern that today's school song repertoire is drawn from a too narrow field of popular music that does not represent students' own listening interests or cultural background, provides unhealthy or unrealistic voice ideals, and is developmentally inappropriate. A recent national evaluation of music teaching (2015) suggested that time and resources allocated to singing may be shrinking and called for further research. In light of these issues, a systematic overview of current song repertoire and how it is used would be an important tool for researchers and teachers.
My doctoral study aims to describe current song repertoire and singing practices in Swedish compulsory schools and to set these findings in a European and historical ethnomusicological perspective. Data was collected through a survey of music teachers (n=302), conducted on a national level between April and September 2016; in a mixed-mode questionnaire, participants provided a complete list of songs sung during the 2015/2016 school year with a chosen grade (grade 4), as well as information such as chosen key, sources of repertoire, and other issues surrounding repertoire selection and classroom singing. Initial findings reveal the complexity of contemporary musical culture in the classroom. The results will be analyzed according to such factors as vocal range, genre, musical content, lyrical content, and country of origin. These findings will be compared with archival material such as song books, textbooks, broadcasts and recordings, to consider current repertoire and teaching practices in an historical ethnomusicological perspective.

Anna Maria Kalcher (Mozarteum University Salzburg)

## "Schmiede Hallein": An Interdisciplinary Cultural Project as Inspiration and Model for Music Education

In Hallein, a town close to Salzburg, a very interesting artistic project has been taking place for some years now. About 250 artists from different fields come together for ten days to create new and innovative works, to learn from each other and from other domains. Concepts and performances are inductively developed and most of them use multimedia. All artists work in the former saline mining facility turned into a cultural venue, an inspiring creative environment, where ideas come into play. This way of designing and making art could also apply to music education. How experiences of this project can be translated into teaching and learning processes will be part of the debate.
It is obvious that new strategies and conditions must be found to realize such adventures. The challenges schools and other institutions face in music education are their formal character, strict guidelines and framework requirements but also different motivational aspects of their students. One possibility is to search for principles and qualities which characterize the cultural project "Schmiede" and are also identifiable in existing music education conceptions. For example, characteristic traits of the Elemental Music and Dance Pedagogy as conceived by Carl Orff and Gunild Keetman emphasize the connection between music, movement, speech and other media, as well as cooperation and, most notably, creative productions.
In my paper I will refer to themes that might inspire music education in schools to become more multimodal, collaborative and artistically focussed. Alternative roles of teachers, such as presenters and mentors, seem to be just as conducive as a well-fitting learning-architecture or the search for new teaching and learning places with a creative laboratory-atmosphere. Following theoretical research and qualitative interviews with participating artists of the "Schmiede", there are indications that this project offers new ideas that initiate and foster cultural learning.

Vaike Kiik-Salupere / Marylin Tilga (Tallinn University)

## What Singing Students Expect from Their Studio Teacher During One-to-One Singing Lessons and How Formal Music Teachers' Education Can Be Improved

Contemporary education has to take into account changes in society and has to be prepared more precisely to meet the requirements of the wide range of learners. One way to find out about the music learners' real interest is to investigate informal music studio work and to take elements of informal education and apply them to the formal education program. According to Elliott (1995) the continuous improvement of teachers as musicians and the refining of the curriculum are the most significant lifelong challenges in music education.
The aim of the study is to reveal
(1) why singing students of different ages choose informal singing lessons in music studios and
(2) what singing students expect from the one-to-one lessons.
In the pilot survey of singing students of different ages an original structured questionnaire was used, including 31 statements, one multiple-choice question, one yes/no question and four open ended questions. The respondents (n=45) were one-to-one singing lesson students from three well recognized private singing studios in Estonia. The questionnaires were delivered in October 2016. Statistical analysis of the data is scheduled for November and its interpretation for December 2016. The results will be finalized by the end of January 2017.
The results of the investigation will indicate which approaches can be applied in music education institutions in order to help contemporary music teachers develop the voice of students of different ages. Informal singing studios afford us direct knowledge
(1) about singing interest of people of different ages and
(2) aspects the modern music teacher should be well prepared for.
Music education institutions have to consider the application of a variety of teaching approaches in the formal music education curriculum.

Ute Konrad / Andreas Lehmann-Wermser (University of Music, Drama and Media, Hannover)

## Linking Theory Building to Classroom Intervention: A Design-Based Research Study on Construction of Meaning

In Germany, music curricula at all stages seek information about musical cultures. This may be conceptualized as introduction and orientation by construction of meaning. At the same time, there is concurrently a strong move towards musical practice in lessons (Jank, 2013). This refers to general music education as well as "Instrumentalklassenunterricht" (instrumental practice and ensemble lessons) aiming at the evocation of music learning in all its facets through the association of theoretical and practical music learning. However, in reality such classes often focus on imparting the skills to play musical instruments without making allowances for aesthetic learning in the sense mentioned above. Based on this comprehension, we had the scholarly interest to develop an evidence-based design, which facilitates cultural learning in practical music lessons in order to generate theoretical knowledge about such processes in such contexts. Within the scope of the design-based research methodology (McKenney & Reeves, 2012), we conducted a complex combined video and audio survey with several video-perspectives, picking individual soundtracks for each student and teacher with the help of clip-on microphones. Therefore, it was possible to analyse non-verbal and verbal interactions on various levels. We observed negotiations about meanings by the pupil parallel to the ongoing lesson which may be labelled as 'backstage processes' (Goffman, 2006). However, such processes are not being used by the teachers to modify their approach of the construction of meanings on a broader basis. In our presentation we will introduce a concept to facilitate such cultural learning processes as described above. We developed this model based on our research results, which we will illustrate with video examples taken from the study.

**John Kratus (Tarpon Springs)**

## Martin Buber in the Music Classroom

The purpose of this session is to apply the ideas of the 20th century German philosopher Martin Buber (1878–1965) to music education. Buber's primary works *I and Thou* (1923) and *Between Man and Man* (1947) outlined a means for human interaction that offers profound implications for music education.

Buber wrote: "Any education worthy of the name is the education of character." Education, he believed, required the exploration and development of two autonomous instincts:

(1) the originative instinct, which is self-knowledge and knowledge of the world, and

(2) the communion instinct, which is the sharing with others.

The originative instinct is creativity. But creativity is not enough, because students need to also share what they create with others. According to Buber an "[...] education based only on the training of the instinct of origination would prepare a new human solitariness which would be the most painful of all."

As applied to music education, Buber's ideas suggest that our classrooms become communities, that our assignments become challenges, that our autocratic teaching becomes dialogic, and that our subject-centered curricula become student-led.

In practical terms, the role of the music teacher becomes one of providing an environment in which students can create and share their musical ideas with others. This is quite different from a classroom in which the teacher corrects students' musical errors.

The session ends with examples of students sharing their musical creations with other students.

**Valerie Krupp-Schleußner (University of Music, Drama and Media, Hannover)**

## Social Justice and the Capability Approach: Theoretical and Empirical Accounts in the Context of Music Education

Many music education projects all over the word are inspired by or directly connected to the Venezuelan project El-Sistema. Increasing social justice and inclusion, creating enthusiasm among participants to express themselves through musical means and giving them a chance for developing musicianship and musical agency are only some of the goals that all those projects share, besides the general hope of educating democratic citizens. Apart from social justice, wellbeing and identity appear to be central concepts framing the discourse.

This paper addresses the question, how social justice and wellbeing in the context of El-Sistema could be seen from a capability perspective, based on Amartya Kumar Sen's and Martha Craven Nussbaum's capability approach. From a practical philosophical view, the approach frames social justice as a function of individual capability and wellbeing, the latter being understood as people's satisfaction with life in general or with respect to certain areas of life. The concept of agency is closely connected to the idea of giving people a chance to live the life they have reason to value (Aristotelian idea of a 'good life') and of developing just societies. The theoretical accounts will be illustrated by empirical results from a study on a music education project in German primary schools. Applying the approach and integrating the children's individual wellbeing can help to overcome the traditional dichotomy of participation and non-participation to which researchers traditionally refer: Four different profiles of participation which depend on the children's musical participation and their wellbeing with respect to their musical capability will be presented; these profiles will be described in-depth by using quantitative data as well as the results from a qualitative content analysis. The results show the children's wellbeing is a useful additional indicator with respect to the investigation and evaluation of music education projects.

**Cristina Marin (University of Music and Performing Arts Graz)**

## Learning a Musical Instrument at School: Frameworks of Cooperation between Music Schools and Regular Schools in Styria

Contexts and structures of formal musical teaching undergo changes in Austria nowadays. Instrumental teachers at music schools encounter new basic conditions for which they did not receive enough or even any training during their studies at a music university. One of these new challenges is the cooperation between music schools and regular schools, mostly in the form of all-day schools, in which the instrumental teacher is required to teach large groups of children and to collaborate with the primary school teacher. In some cases, adding to this problem, questions of feasibility and cooperation cannot be answered. This situation and the lack of appropriate training may lead to refusal, stress and burnout amongst instrumental teachers.

The aim of this study is to analyse the current situation of cooperation between music schools and regular schools in the region of Styria (Austria) from the perspective of its stakeholders. To do so we carried out interviews with music school teachers, directors and policy makers of this region. By means of a qualitative content analysis we developed a system of inductive categories through which we identified and systematised the main topics addressed by the interviewees. These topics referred to the political situation regarding all-day schools, the possible forms of cooperation between music schools and all-day schools at different structural levels – between institutions and between teachers – and the structural and pedagogical characteristics of current cooperation projects.

Two main conclusions, among others, can be drawn from this study. First, political decisions are urgently needed in order to solve the situation of coexistence of music schools and all-day schools. Second, the economic resources allocated for the cooperation projects and the interest of policy makers in such projects are determinant for their proper functioning and ultimately for their teaching and learning quality.

**Jelena Martinovic Bogojevic (University of Montenegro, Cetinje)**

## A National Project Supporting the Development of Music Pedagogy in Montenegro

The Ministry of Science and Ministry of Culture of Montenegro funded the national project "Identity Elements in Montenegrin Music as a Basis for Development of Multiculturalism and Interculturalism" which was implemented by the Music Academy between 2012 and 2015. The project was primarily focused on music pedagogy and affirmation of music folklore with the younger population. During the implementation of the project, we cooperated with multiple institutions, which contributed to the productivity of researchers and the achievement of projected goals. As an example of best practice, we encouraged the formation of vocal ensembles and the organization of concerts in many towns within Montenegro. Music written to reflect folklore themes formed the center of attention of the presentations. Furthermore, a textbook for initial solfeggio classes in music schools was published. The work of young composers was encouraged and a collection of piano compositions was published. In this study, we will present some of the key elements of the project, which were implemented through the cooperation with music schools, the Institute for Textbooks and Teaching Aids in Podgorica, and Centers of Culture in Bar and Tivat. External input was achieved through participation in international symposiums on music pedagogy held in: Istanbul, Pula, Split, Sarajevo and Belgrade. An interesting feature of this project is that many institutions were networking during its implementation, cooperating with the aim of promoting music culture and a process of affirmation of the musical heritage among the younger population.

**Wolfgang Mastnak (University of Music and Performing Arts, Munich)**

## The Wealth of Mental Diversity: Psychopathological Challenges of Music in Schools

Music in classroom education is full of psychopathological issues such as suicide, schizophrenia, and depression illustrated in opera, the German Lied, and other musical genres. Given that some pupils might be at psychopathological risks or have manifested psychiatric and/or psychosomatic diagnoses, this can involve the potential for both fatal outcomes in music classes or valuable benefits for self-discovery and self-regulation. A lack of awareness of dangerous situations and conditions can make the music educational process a trigger of the pupil's self-destruction, depressive despair, or (pseudo-)psychotic fits. However, awareness by teachers can greatly support and prevent psychosomatic issues, enhance personal growth, and facilitate therapeutic processes.

Additionally, musical creativity and uniqueness are often inextricably intertwined with unusual thinking and abnormal minds and can conflict with modes of regular education. These talents might cause issues that lead to traumatisation, both in the sense of vulnerability and aggressive behaviour.

Understanding inventiveness in a holistic way reveals the multifaceted potential of arts-based education that includes both the development of the artistic self and prevention of education-based pathogenesis. This concerns not only pupils with psychiatric diagnoses or pathological dispositions, but also educational modes that suppress the growth of the self and disorders that are an immediate result of classroom-experiences.

In contrast to common views of abnormity and psychiatric diagnoses that derive from socio-cultural evolution and cognitive-behavioral approaches, music provides an unlimited space for inventive play, discovery, expression, and self-realisation. So called pathological features such as various forms of hallucinations might become the source of creative acts. Music in educational settings can enhance empathetic understanding and arts-based skills of self-regulation and hence control pathological developments. In this context the integration of the arts and improvisation play a crucial role and involve the theory and practice of Polyaesthetic Education.

**Tobias Emanuel Mayer (Ludwig-Maximilians-Universität München)**

## The Bernstein-Effect: Stars of Classical Music as 'Infectious' Classroom Music Educators

Like Leonard Bernstein, who set a milestone in music education with his "Young People's Concerts", today's stars of classical music visit schools to bring their musical enthusiasm to the classroom. In my presentation, I will share the key findings of my research project regarding the Bernstein-Effect, maintaining that stars of classical music as music educators are able to spark young people's interest in classical music (even if they do not have any affinity to classical music). So what are the benefits for schools and teachers in engaging in joint (ad)ventures with famous musicians?
The evaluation of the empirical studies with the stars of classical music Daniel Müller-Schott (cello), Martin Stadtfeld (piano), Evgenia Rubinova (piano) and Arabella Steinbacher (violin) can provide an answer. Each musician visited a German high school with about one hundred 13 to 16 year old pupils; the logistics of this project were partially facilitated by "Rhapsody in School". Based on quantitative surveys with a pre-, post- and follow-up online questionnaire including music samples, an increased interest of the pupils could be observed regarding liking and listening to classical music. This methodological approach was complemented by qualitative interviews with the stars of classical music and teachers including audio-visual documentation of the school visits.
The key result is a newly gained openness of young people concerning classical music. In this context the star of classical music plays a more significant role as a musician rather than as a star. Thus, he succeeds as a music educator, especially due to his musical performance, in creating a musical encounter and therefore enabling access to classical music for the pupils. The Bernstein-Effect can become a window of opportunity for young people, so that they can get and stay in touch with classical music.

**Dale Misenhelter (University of Arkansas, Fayetteville)**

## Pre-Service Teacher Perceptions of Interdisciplinary Teaching

Recommendations toward interdisciplinary teaching are common across many age levels, schools, and learning communities. Provisions for guidelines regarding content and strategies are not frequently specified, and a variety of perceptions and pedagogical understandings may result, particularly among younger teachers in training. Sometimes referred to as extra-musical, integrated, or collaborative teaching, the lack of specificity can be problematic if for no other reason than the lack of defining terminology. Hirsch (2002) describes at some length the problem of vague definitions in education across a society, while Marc (2015) suggests that interdisciplinary and comparative studies are necessary for a nuanced understanding of cultural learning and creativity.
In this study, pre-service tertiary (undergraduate) students (N=64) at two comprehensive universities provided responses to questions regarding their understanding of
(1) the expression 'interdisciplinary';
(2) synonymous terms;
(3) extra-musical outcomes and activities.
Written responses were collected during coursework, with questioning intended to promote reflection and further pedagogical consideration.
Participant definitions of interdisciplinary teaching were nearly evenly distributed among two broad categories: shared subject matter (48.3%), and confounded associations with classroom management (51.7%). Synonymous terms from the first category included "collaborative, adventurous, combined, comprehensive, connecting, expanding" etc., while misidentified associations in the second category included "self-control, rules, consequences, behavior, and punishment."

Responses in regard to 'extra-musical' included 'historical context, learning languages, problem solving, analysis skills, social and cooperative skills, mnemonic devices, and music therapy' etc. Students also commonly identified cultural and generational connections, as well as building familiarity with music with which they might otherwise not have come into contact.
As suggested by the wide ranging responses, many undergraduate teachers in training seem to lack clear understanding of interdisciplinary teaching, and perhaps as a result, have minimal consequent plans to utilize broader creative teaching in the arts. Increased exposure in university training seems warranted.

**Gwen Moore (University of Limerick)**

## "Musical Futures" in Ireland: Findings from a Pilot Study

Since Green's (2002) seminal publication on how popular musicians learn, significant change has occurred within music curricula and pedagogy in international contexts to include informal and non-formal learning approaches. "Musical Futures" has been incorporated into schools across the UK, US, Canada, Australia and Brazil. Despite the celebrated success of Irish popular musicians in public discourse, Irish educational policy has tended to overlook popular music in favor of Western classical and Irish traditional music genres. This paper reports on a pilot study of the "Musical Futures" approach in Ireland. Three secondary schools and two primary schools piloted this approach over the course of a school term. A mixed methods approach underpinned the methodology for the study which included a survey questionnaire of teachers and pupils in addition to in depth semi-structured interviews with music teachers and focus groups with the pupils. Findings resonate with previous "Musical Futures" studies internationally, for example, motivation for learning, developing critical listening and ensemble skills, and enthusiasm for music as a subject. However, similarities were found in the informal learning practices and associated skills between popular and Irish traditional music practices. The paper will consider the implications of the study for impending curricular changes at secondary level in Ireland. In addition, the paper will contextualize the findings for bicultural/multicultural contexts nationally and internationally and make recommendations for incorporating Musical Futures in similar contexts.

**Irena Müller-Brozovic (University of Arts Berne)**

## 'Lost and Found'. The Focus on Music in Concerts within a Mediating Context: The Theoretical Framework of a Planned Case Study

Music mediation in concerts aims at filling the gap between the audience and (an unfamiliar) music and at intensifying the relationship between music and listeners. Therefore music mediation modifies the traditional concert: There are new concert settings, contexts, venues, irritations as well as interactive, interdisciplinary and multimedial approaches. But do they actually help to get acquainted with an unfamiliar music and to focus on the music? These doubts lead to the research question: How can musicians and music mediators, by applying a reflected method, facilitate the focus of recipients in concerts on music? What is 'focus on music'? What music bound methods of mediation are there? What preconditions, requirements and criteria for music bound methods facilitate or impede a focus on music?
The current state of the research suggests a theoretic framework of music mediation in concerts. The PhD-thesis aims – with a case study yet to be done – at formulating questions as a guideline for musicians and music mediators for preparing and realizing concerts within a context of music mediation. The results of the research are intended to contribute to reflected praxes (Elliott/Silverman, 2015) and the professionalization of music mediation.
The concert is conceived as a situation of intense music perception and a situation of transformation (Anders, 1926/27). Captivation (Brown/Nowak, 2007) is key to an open attitude towards music. The audience then establishes and intensifies relationships with, to and in music (Rosa, 2016). Schmid (2014) describes different ways of experiencing music. Some methods of music mediating celebrate and dramatize music (Rebstock, 2009), others help to understand music (Richter, 2012). Performativity (Fischer-Lichte, 2012) and aesthetic transformation (Brandstätter, 2013) both open a liminal space where transformative educational processes (Koller, 2012) are triggered.
A focus on music understood as an intense and vibrating relationship or resonance with, to and in music cannot be planned. The research mentions favourable and impeding factors for a focus on music.

Ertem Nalbantoglu (Near East University, Nicosia) / Sharon Lierse (Charles Darwin University, Australia)

## Music Education in the Northern Part of Cyprus and Australia: A Joint (Ad)venture in Music

Music is a universal form of communication in which cultures have developed their own traditions. The northern part of Cyprus and Australia are at the opposite sides of the planet but are both islands that have been influenced by their own respective dominant cultures; that is the British colonization of Australia up until the 1950s and Turkey after 1974 for North Cyprus.
Both, the northern part of Cyprus an Australia have universities which offer specialized courses in training music educators. They also have a school curriculum which includes music. It is through this joint (ad)venture that music in the curriculum will be examined to understand how it reflects and perpetuates the regions' unique culture.
The northern part of Cyprus has recently completed a revised national music education curriculum for elementary schools whereby all government and private schools have to follow each unit. Teachers' handbooks (2006, 2016) have been widely used for the last decade in order to help teachers with teaching methods, children's songs and music taught in the classroom.
Australia has recently developed a national curriculum from Foundation Year to Grade 10. Known as ACARA, the Australian Curriculum, Assessment and Reporting Authority includes music as one of the five arts subjects (Australian Curriculum, Assessment and Reporting Authority, 2016). The curriculum is generalized and teachers are largely free to develop their own syllabus. There is no set music education textbook, nor are there easily accessible resources on local Australian music. An issue is how, if at all, Australia's identity and culture is manifested through its musical traditions.
The purpose of the paper is to compare and contrast these two systems to gain a better understanding of how music education is taught and represented in the primary years. Through the joint (ad)venture, themes and issues are discussed in order to better understand the musical culture and how it can be incorporated in the local curriculum.

Susan O'Neill / Yaroslav Senshyn (Simon Fraser University, Vancouver)

## Enhancing Learners' Engagement in Collaborative Practices in the Music Classroom through a Focus on Reciprocity

A growing number of researchers have identified the need for studies examining the nature and influence of relationships that enhance learners' engagement in collaborative music activities. And yet, the literature provides few reciprocal explanatory frameworks for examining engaged collaborative processes. This paper therefore draws on the concept of reciprocity within Actor-Network Theory as a theoretical lens for interpreting learners' engagement in collaborative music activities. A study of 44 Grade 7 students' collaborative music learning practices was undertaken by observing video recordings of small groups of four to six students while they engaged in collaborative music activities during their regular music classes over a ten-week period. A coding procedure was developed and used to examine reciprocal behaviours and collaborative processes over time. The results showed how learners' engagement was constituted through relationships with their instruments, the various tools they were using to assist their learning, and their social practices. The notion of collaboration as happening merely between students was challenged as the musical and material resources they were engaging with were found important for enhancing engagement in the sense that they entailed or enacted and energized their collaborative music practices. The findings are presented in the form of a mediation model:

(1) when students were united in the meanings and actions of what they were working on because
(2) they understood the social uses of what they were learning in relation to the material resources they were engaging with,
(3) this contributed to the stability and focus of their collaborative music practices which
(4) enhanced their music engagement and learning. Also, students who were identified by their teachers as being less engaged during regular music classes were often highly engaged and positioned by their peers as knowledgeable during small group collaborations.

Implications for enhancing learners' engagement in the music classroom will be discussed.

**Dora Psaltopoulou-Kamini / Evangelia Chatziioannidou (Aristotle University of Thessaloniki-Greece)**

## Fundamental Training in Music Therapy Encourages Significant Changes in Music Students

Music therapy training encourages music students to discover new paths relating to people with special needs through music, as well as to explore new ways of using music, opening paths to self and music growth (Nordoff & Robbins, 1965 & 2007; Psaltopoulou, 2012, 2013 & 2015).

The purpose of this study was to explore the experiences of musicology students who had fundamental music therapy training, attended a community music therapy performance and spoke with the parents of the performers with special needs.

A phenomenological-hermeneutic design was adopted for this study. Semi-structured interviews which ranged from 45 to 60 minutes were conducted with 52 students. They were encouraged to share their experience in their own words and helped to illuminate the richness and complexity of vivid experiences with their answers to open-ended questions, developed without any predesigned hypothesis. Data analysis was undertaken by three independent researchers and guided by Diekelmann, Allen and Tanner's (1989) phenomenological technique, which includes a seven-stage process. Triangulation techniques were used to ascertain the credibility and trustworthiness of findings.

The students reported that they understood the important role of the use of music concerning non musical and musical goals for people with disabilities in music therapy and/or in community music therapy. They referred to significantly positive changes in their perceptions about people with special needs and they discovered meaningful ways to effectively relate to them through music. They also enriched their own self expression and growth through and in music, as well as they found ways to deal with stage fright. They all found the training very helpful for music education, composition and performing.

A fundamental music therapy training integrated into curricula for music education, composition and/or performing studies can effectively contribute to the musician's growth whether he/she will become a music therapist or not.

**Johannes van der Sandt (Free University of Bozen-Bolzano)**

## 'Oh Boy!' Boys' Choirs: Do They Still Matter?

With ongoing debates as to whether single-gender education is advantageous for boys, and research on the missing males in choirs problem, this presentation's purpose is to explore the perceived benefits and values for boys singing in the world-renowned Drakensberg Boys' Choir, and to establish an educational basis for the existence of boys' choirs. Worldwide there are many boys' choirs, but the Drakensberg Boys' Choir is one of only a few of its kind: selected from a residential boys' choir school using choral music as a significant vehicle for holistic education. Semi-structured questionnaires were given to choristers, known as Drakies, to ascertain their perceptions of their choir membership. Their experiences are noted in terms of musical, social and behavioral skills gained. The main emerging themes in each category are discussed in order to lay claim to the assumption that boys' choirs exist not only to entertain, nor are their goals purely musical or pedagogical. They can rather be regarded as unique cultural artifacts that aid boys' development into well-equipped and well-rounded young men. Boys' choirs are instruments that are irrevocably part of musical culture; however, the structure, composition and functions of choirs, networking and partnerships need to be reconsidered in order to lay claim to the validity of boys' choirs as important music educational instruments, and not only instruments kept alive for the sake of sentiment and tradition. Administrational and artistic directors of boys' choirs need to think creatively and freshly to establish partnerships that make their instruments socially and educationally relevant in an ever-changing society. The findings of the study that will be presented are the result of field and online research as well as a literature survey to identify possible interdisciplinary and multimedia approaches to ensure the credibility, longevity and relevancy of boys' choirs.

Johannes van der Sandt (Free University of Bozen-Bolzano)

## Community Singing: A Pathway to Social Capital – a Cross-Cultural Comparative Assessment of the Benefits of Singing Communities in South Tyrol and South Africa

This quantitative study investigates different approaches of community singing in building social capital in South Tyrol, Italy and South Africa. The impact of the various approaches of community singing is examined by investigating the main components of social capital, namely, social norms and obligations, social networks and associations and trust, and how these components are manifested in two different societies. The research is based on the premise that community singing is an important agent for the development of social capital. It seeks to establish in what form community singing can best enhance the social capital of communities in South Tyrol that are undergoing significant changes in the ways in which social capital is generally being generated on account of demographic, economic, technological and cultural changes. By comparing the different approaches to community singing in two multicultural societies I hope to gain insight, and an understanding of the connections between culture, social cohesion, identity and therefore to be able to add to the understanding of the building of social capital through community singing. There is a growing body of research to suggest that participation in music may contribute to the accumulation and accessibility of social capital in a community. In sociological discourses on social capital generation the dimension of community music making is recognized as an important factor. Social capital evolves as a shared resource of trust and reciprocity when people listen to each other, work or play together, and care about each other. Trust, shared norms and values civic and community involvement, networks, knowledge resources, contact with families and friends, and fellowship are key components in fostering group cohesion and social capital development in a community. The research will show that there is no better place for these factors to flourish than in a community singing group.

Helmut Schaumberger (Mozarteum University Salzburg)

## The Professional Director of Children's Choirs and Youth Choirs: Findings of a Study on Special Training Courses in Austria

In 2010, the first in-service training course for directors of children's choirs and youth choirs started at Mozarteum University Salzburg. Since then, around 30 students graduated from this two year course that was developed in co-operation with the Vienna Boys' Choir. Most graduates could subsequently start a career as professional conductors/directors of children's and youth choirs; this testifies the quality of this training.

In 2014, Helmut Schaumberger, assistant for music pedagogy at Mozarteum University Salzburg, started his PhD-research project on the professionalization of special training courses for directors of children's and youth choirs. In addition to a description of the characteristics of a professional director of children's and youth choirs, he started a survey among professional Austrian directors. The aim of this qualitative study was to find new categories for the further development of training courses.

In the first part of his project report, Helmut Schaumberger focuses on the 'director of children's and youth choirs' and presents various perspectives and connotations. Furthermore, he delineates the work area of directors and discusses the strongly varied age-limits of children's and youth choirs and the consequences that result from the special training courses. In the last part of his presentation, he develops a model of competences for the directors of children's choirs and youth choirs based on current findings in music pedagogy and teacher training.

Gabriele Schellberg (University of Passau)

## How Musical Do Primary Generalist Student Teachers Consider Themselves?

In Germany, most of the music lessons in primary schools are taught by generalist teachers, who had little or no musical training within their teacher education program and therefore lack self-confidence in teaching music (Holden & Button, 2006; Schellberg, 2016). Classroom teachers may be the sole providers of music instruction for primary school pupils (Della Pietra, 2010). Researchers hold a strong belief that self-perceptions provide a basic foundation for behavior (Vannatta-Hall, 2010). In the domain of music education, teachers' self-efficacy can directly affect the number and types of musical experiences teachers provide for their students (Battersby & Cave, 2014). According to

Ritchie & Williamon (2011) prior music experiences and participation are the highest predictors of music self-efficacy for learning. Therefore, the basic aim of my study was to find out about prior musical experiences of the students in our teacher education programme in Bavaria. How musical do these student teachers consider themselves? How does this assessment relate to students' prior musical experiences?
To explore these questions a study was designed. A questionnaire at the beginning of the semester focused on the reasons why the students had not selected music as a special subject in their teacher training programme; on their previous musical experiences (instrument, chorus) and on their memories of music lessons in primary school (n=466). The questionnaire was complemented by a short musical biography (n=142).
The results of my research refer to people who had been influential in the childhood and adolescence of my test persons and to experiences with music mainly gained in primary school and in secondary school music lessons as well as in private music lessons. The data show that primary generalist student teachers bring rich experiences of music and music-making into their teacher education programmes. However, many participants do not consider themselves as musical despite of having played an instrument for several years. Obviously it is necessary to make them aware of their musicality and increase the skills they have already acquired.

**Jason Silveira (University of Oregon, Eugene) / Jacob Close (Ithaca College, New York)**

## Music Education in Transition: Providing Support for Transgender Music Students

There has been increased attention focusing on transgender individuals and challenges they face in society and in schools specifically (e.g. Braw, 2014; Morris, 2015; Silveira & Goff, 2016; Thompson, 2015). Additionally, EAS has called for researchers to support young people's self-determined cultural lives and foster cooperative projects between schools and other institutions. This research paper aims to address that call. Transgender students are disproportionately frequent targets of harassment, also on part of school staff and teachers. This observation points at the need to investigate teachers' roles in creating safer environments for sexual minorities. We investigate the challenges of one gender-variant music student and his experiences as a music education major in college as a pre-service music teacher. This study uses an adaptation of the D'Augelli (1994) lifespan model of sexual orientation identity development to investigate the lived experiences of a transgender music education student at an American college. A semi-structured interview protocol was used, with approximately 14 weekly one-on-one meetings with the student, including personal artifacts provided by the student. Data were coded based on recurring patterns that emerged from the interviews and artifacts. Member checks and a peer examiner were used to ensure faithful interpretation of the data.
The following themes emerged:
(1) Identity construction within the School of Music proved difficult because of a lack of faculty support;
(2) certain curricular aspects (e.g., concert attire, student teaching placements, applying for jobs) were stress inducing;
(3) internalized trans-phobia eventually gave way to identity development;
(4) money turned out as a barrier to identity development; and
(5) the student was open to sharing strategies to support his personal and professional needs.
Implications for music teacher preparation programs and professional development will be discussed. Suggestions on how university faculty, music teachers, and music teacher educators can provide individual, curricular, and institutional support for transgender music students will be shared.

**Persefoni Tzanaki (University of Sheffield)**

## The Impact of Empathy on Social Rhythmic Entrainment in Children's Musical Interaction: Cognitive and Motor-Emotional Approaches

Social rhythmic entrainment, understood as the temporal coordination of children's music-making as well as their affective connection during their musical interaction, is a demanding skill. It has been associated with empathy promoted by the synchronisation of the emotional states of individuals (Rabinowitch et al., 2013). However, less attention has been paid to the impact of empathy on rhythmic entrainment, although personality traits are considered highly influential parameters of musical interpersonal coordination. In addition, the significance of the specific type of musical interaction on the impact of empathy remains unclear.

The aim of the research presented here is to investigate

(1) to which degree empathy influences children's rhythmic entrainment during their musical interaction,
(2) how two different approaches of musical activities (cognitive vs. motor-emotional) contribute to the impact of empathy.

In total, 40 children were recruited from British primary schools. They were chosen according to their scores in the empathy questionnaire "Feeling-Thinking" by Garton & Gringart (2005). A pre-test ensured that all participants had similar personal rhythmic skills. The experiments included fun rhythmic activities with claves and body percussion and children's tapping was measured by electronic drum-pads.

Descriptive analyses indicated that groups with high empathy were better entrained than groups with low empathy. In addition, groups that participated in the cognitive approach of activities were less entrained than groups in the motor-emotional approach. Similar results were stated for the affective entrainment of groups.

These results are in line with studies which highlight the role of Mirror Neuron System and the process of motor simulation during rhythmic entrainment (Novembre et al., 2014). These observations support the conclusion that children with better ability to perceive the others' actions via their enhanced empathic ability can be better temporally and affectively entrained with their co-performers as they better anticipate and perceive the others' actions. Activities with motor-emotional approach seem to facilitate these processes.

**Jonas Völker (Hochschule für Musik Freiburg)**

## Multicultural Music Learning with Percussion Instruments: A Design-Based Research Study

Because of the emerging flow of refugees in Germany since the summer of 2015, the educational sector has been facing new opportunities and challenges. To accommodate the changing social reality in the educational institutions, it is necessary to develop applicable innovative concepts of multicultural learning. Especially since music education has the potential to play a vital role in preparing students for the multicultural life in German society by exposing them to diversity and cultural heterogeneity (Barth, 2008).

An examination of the discourse "Multicultural Music Education" in German speaking countries shows that on the one hand, there is an emphasis on conceptual deliberation and the development of lesson-specific material. On the other hand, there is barely any corresponding research activity taking into account the theoretical or empirical issues (Knigge, 2012).

Inspired by the design-based research approach (Reinmann, 2005), I will study how multicultural teaching and learning with percussion instruments can lead to a musical and practical access and foster reflection on diverse musical cultures. Therefore, I will examine learning circumstances not in a laboratory, but in real-life music lessons. Through this, my research will deliver an inside view of students' reflections about multicultural topics. Furthermore, didactical scenarios about multicultural music learning with percussion instruments will be developed which prove practically beneficial to multicultural music lessons. It is the goal to reach a general design solution through methodical structuring, realisation, validating and re-designing (Prediger et al., 2012).

In my presentation, I will show the concept and first results of my study and describe my research approach.

# PRACTICE PAPERS

**Katharina Anzengruber (Mozarteum University Salzburg)**

## "KLANGKÖRPER – KÖRPERKLANG". Experimenting with Sounds: An Interdisciplinary Approach to Teaching Arts and Natural Sciences

Which sounds can be produced on / with / through different 'bodies'? What does the human body sound like? How do different objective bodies sound? How do sounds emerge? How do we perceive them? ... These and further questions are dealt with by 50 pupils between the age of 15 and 17, who attend an Austrian grammar school, in cooperation with artists such as scientists within an interdisciplinary project named "KLANGKÖRPER – KÖRPERKLANG", taking place from January 2017 until July 2017. Within this project the pupils are continuously confronted with different sound generators and sounds from the perspective of art and from the perspective of natural science. In this context the experiment itself functions as a kind of methodological principle with central significance. This project is part of a longitudinal study, which is implemented within a PhD project, and focuses on the scientific examination (documentation, analysis and evaluation) of pupils' learning processes and processes of (aesthetic) experience, developing from their work on experimental art forms. Additionally, it is an aim to find out what 'experimental' teaching in art education should look like. In this context it is interesting to look at those subjects where the experiment has 'tradition': the natural sciences. Within the presentation, an insight into the project "KLANGKÖRPER – KÖRPERKLANG" will be given. Furthermore, first results concerning the accompanying empirical study will be presented. These are some questions which are going to be discussed: How should 'experimental' teaching be exercised? Do conventional teaching structures permit this way of teaching? What are the differences between experimenting within science and arts education? Why should pupils work on experimental art forms at school? What is the role of experimental art forms for educational theory looking to initiate processes of (aesthetic) experience and creative behavior?

**Andreas Bernhofer / Monika Oebelsberger (Mozarteum University Salzburg) / Petra Brüderl (Mozarteum Foundation)**

## Joint Venture: University – School – Festival

For the past 15 years music-education students have been developing workshops to organize classical concerts, which take place during the course of 'MOZART Woche' and are accessible to a young audience. This concept led to a successful and enduring cooperation between two institutions: MOZARTEUM University Salzburg and MOZARTEUM Foundation Salzburg. Although these institutions share the same name, they pursue different goals. The Mozarteum University Salzburg provides a well-grounded music teacher education, both science-based and practice-oriented; while the Salzburg Mozarteum Foundation is a non-profit organization whose primary focus encompasses the life and œuvre of Wolfgang Amadé Mozart. The organization offers concerts, maintains the 'Mozart Museum' and supports academic research. The collaboration of these two institutions led to a practice-oriented course for prospective music teachers. In this course, graduate students have the task to develop, organize and put into practice workshops for middle and high school students. In the meantime several schools Have become 'third' partners in this fruitful joint (ad)venture. Within these workshops, which take place in the schools, the pupils are introduced to the classical concerts they are going to attend. The challenge was on the one hand to get the young people in touch with the music in an active and motivating way and on the other hand – to acquaint the students with out-of-school cultural bodies and to make them realize the benefits of cooperation. The workshop development was fostered by different impulses from the course instructors (e.g. different didactical concepts, concert experiences by a young audience). In our session, we want to present two different things: We want to show you the development of this cooperation as a wonderful example for a win-win situation for all involved partners. In addition, the students of the last course will join us and explain their workshop concepts for the "Mozartwoche 2016" and talk about their experiences.

**Arkadiusz Bialak (LASALLE College of the Arts, Singapore)**

## Learning Elementary Harmony and Keyboard Skills through a Collaborative Approach

The participants of this project are comprised of a group of classical piano students attending the "Keyboard Skills" module at Singapore LASALLE College of the Arts during their first academic year of the BA- programme. All the participating students have obtained ABRSM Grade 8 or an equivalent. There are two principal aims of the quoted module. The first one is to enhance the students' mastery of the keyboard geography. The second, perhaps more important one, involves enhanced familiarization with the basic concepts of functional harmony. These skills are closely aligned with other BA course modules and are crucial in developing sound musicianship. Traditionally, acquisition of harmony-related skills entails delivery of the underlying principles by the teacher and subsequent repetition-based practice by the students. However, such methodology does not necessarily facilitate comprehensive understanding of the learned concepts and ensuing proficiency of their execution. The approach employed by the presenter relies on exposing the students to examples of various music genres (classical, pop, traditional) and asking for recognition of the learned harmonic patterns. Students are also encouraged to provide examples of their choice. The typical class activities include short live performances by the lecturer and students, utilization of audio/video recordings, and discussions. The approach described above brings several benefits. First, it facilitates learning through connecting the newly acquired concepts with the material already known by the students. Secondly, it encourages participants' own research and actively engages them in the process of learning. Thirdly, sharing and explaining own findings to the peers results in an increase of all the participants' knowledge through collaborative learning. Lastly, exchange of knowledge in the atmosphere of cooperation favourably alters the traditionally divisive power hierarchy of the lecturer versus the students which creates a more efficient learning environment and fosters closer bonds between all participants.

**Rainer Brinkmann (Staatsoper im Schiller Theater, Berlin), Anne-Kathrin Ostrop (Komische Oper, Berlin), Monika Oebelsberger (Mozarteum University Salzburg)**

## Joint (Ad)venture Opera

The practice paper will present a successful cooperation – a joint venture – of cultural institutions (Staatsoper, Berlin/ Komische Oper, Berlin), University (Mozarteum University, Salzburg) and an independent cultural institute (ISIM / Institute for Scenic Interpretation of Music and Theater).
Most Opera Houses are setting up cultural initiatives to get people enthusiastic about opera and musical projects. They offer extracurricular music education to people of all ages and professions. Nevertheless there are only a few well trained music educators for this specific field comprising educational and outreaching programs of opera houses. Based on this observation the idea to cooperate was 'born'. We decided to set up a curriculum for graduate students offering a profound training based on the concept of the Scenic Interpretation (Szenische Interpretation). This approach was initially developed at the University of Oldenburg between 1982 and 1990 and since then has been adapted to evolving demands of recent cultural life. In this practice paper the curriculum will be presented and discussed, specific methods of Scenic Interpretation will be worked out in greater detail and some practical examples will be put into practice. Finally the fields of work opening up for graduates will be pointed out.

**Giovanna Carugno (School of the Accademia Filarmonica of Bologna / Italian Society for Music Education)**

## Scarlatti and his Harpsichord: A Mixed Pedagogical Approach to Teaching Music History at Primary School Level

Many studies underline the importance of teaching music history at primary school level and the key role of historical sources and listening activities. This project was conducted with 20 students attending the third class in a primary school in Rome. The project endeavors to establish a mixed pedagogical approach to teaching music history at primary school by finding the right way to stimulate children's curiosity and creativity and make it easier to absorb facts and information. It is based on a pedagogical approach that combines the use of historical sources with storytelling and listening activities and was carried out in two different phases. In phase one, the music teacher held a two-hour lesson dedicated to the composer Domenico Scarlatti, telling the students a magic story about his life and showing them some historical sources (portrait of Scarlatti, copies of manuscripts). This was followed by a listening activity: The children were involved in listening to Scarlatti's keyboard pieces live, played by a professional musician on the harpsichord. In this phase the children had the opportunity to observe the instrument closely and try to play it. After the lesson, the children were asked to draw their favorite activities and to write what they have learned about Scarlatti. The results show that most of the children enjoyed the music history activities and remembered the main information about Scarlatti, his life and works. As a result, some children expressed their interest in repeating the didactic experience and in learning to play the harpsichord.

**Mercedes Castillo-Ferreira (Universidad de Jaén) / Manuel Ángel Puentes-Zamora**

## Sound-Art-Installation at Infant School: Space Music

This paper analyses a learning project in which five year old children designed, developed and built a sound-art-installation in their infant school classroom. Framed in the context of an integrated curriculum and collaborative work, the main aim of the project was to develop their creativity through artistic language, particularly in the field of Sound-Art. Using the sounds of different planets and stars recorded by the NASA Voyager probe as a starting point, the children created four compositions to form part of the artistic installation. Using sounds from different sources such as 'Freesound' (a database of creative common licensed sounds found on the internet) or recorded by themselves, the children learnt how to structure a sound piece. During the process they also worked on vocal improvisations, graphical representations of the sound and musical concepts like texture, dynamics or structure.

**Claudia Cerachowitz (Walddörfer-Gymnasium, Hamburg)**

## Oskar and his Friends: Initiating and Organizing the Development of Music and Arts in School

This lecture will show how cooperation with external cultural institutions can be initiated and organized with the aim of developing artistic and aesthetic education. The work of a music teacher within the structure of a high school in Hamburg is presented as a case study. The lecture will be opened with a response to the question: "What could we as music teachers gain from joint ventures?" The subsequent discussion will point out the requirements for carrying out cooperations with regards to possible benefits and/or objectives.
Part 1 presents the functional levels and fields of action in which specific tasks are defined and organized. These are, for example: (1) the level of the head of the department, (2) the level of 'coordination' of aesthetic subjects, as well as (3) the level of the school's 'cultural objectives'.
In Part 2 project examples serve to illustrate the three functional levels more precisely. The focus is on the aspects 'development of teaching', 'school development' and 'cooperation with external partners'.
Part 3 will inquire into the conditions for the work shown in Part 1 and 2. This results in at least three fields of development, namely: (1) the necessary competencies of musicians in school, (2) the guidelines for personal and organizational development of school, (3) the possibilities of the respective external cultural partner.
The criteria of the model of a "school of arts" (Braun, Fuchs & Kelb, 2013) serve as a theoretical base for this practical example. This will also illustrate the central role that can be played by a music teacher concerning the development of teaching at their school.

**Sunny Choi (New York University)**

## Components Contributing to Development in the Field of Improvisation: Artistic Piano Interpretation of *Lean On*

As the advancement and accessibility to technology has made it easier than ever to create music, the use of multimedial approaches in music education also introduces new challenges and benefits. Finding a healthy balance between the utilization of technological tools and teaching/learning becomes crucial to foster a better understanding of music without letting the tools invade as sources of distraction. In this particular practice research, *Flat*, a web-based music notation software, was used as a tool that assisted with explaining the author's innovative piano improvisation pedagogical approach.

Helping young people to develop a deeper understanding of music can be approached with implementing aural skill development using western popular music, where creativity and diversity are integrated within the curriculum. A piece of music can undergo substantial surface alteration, and yet be recognized as the same piece, such as variation forms in western European classical music and instrumental "covers" of popular music songs that are widely shared today among professional and amateur musicians via social media platforms.

*Lean On*, is a popular music song that belongs to house music genre, written by combination of European and American artists that include a French DJ, a Danish singer and an American producer. Change of instrumentation, embellishment, and other contributing components that make up the improvisation-based version of *Lean On* are actively explored in my practice research for the interpretation process of *Lean On* as a solo piano music rendition.

**Smaragda Chrysostomou (National and Kapodistrian University of Athens)**

## User Generated Content (UGC) Environments Fostering Collaboration to Enrich Music Teaching in Schools

Learning is an inherently social activity. In this current era, collaborative and constructivist learning is particularly augmented by social networks and web 2.0 technologies that place great emphasis on user-generated content, content sharing and collaborative work. Recent developments in Greece related to the incorporation of digital technology in music education include a number of environments/platforms where UGC is not only encouraged but also 'expected' in order for the content to be enriched. Examples of such environments include the 'Photodento' repository, 'Euterpi' and 'Aesop' that have been created as part of large collaborations between various institutions, music educators, music teachers and the Ministry of Education. These novel tools and created environments facilitate music teachers to interact, share and ultimately build learning communities. In this presentation these platforms will be presented and a SWOT-analysis will assist in exploring the advantages of these tools and processes for the teaching and learning of music in schools. As this tsunami of UGC overtakes learning organizations and taps into the social aspect of learning, highlighting its collaborative and creative characteristics, a number of questions are raised: How can users be encouraged to participate? What are the safeguards of quality that need to be in place? How can we prepare for and deal with negative as well as positive engagement? And how can we maximize the benefits from such a collaboration between music teachers, organizations and institutions for the future of music teaching and learning?

**Shirley Day-Salmon (Mozarteum University Salzburg / Orff Institute)**

## Inclusive Music Making

Which types of activity, which instruments or materials, which methods can be beneficial when working with mixed ability groups? This paper presents the principles of inclusive education (Georg Feuser) and the demands of inclusive music making (Wilhelm Keller) and their realization within music and movement sessions with adults of various abilities and disabilities. It concludes with thoughts on their relevance for inclusive music making in schools. Adults with additional support needs from two 'Lebenshilfe'-sheltered workshops attend weekly music and movement sessions at the Orff Institute, Mozarteum University for one or sometimes many years. The sessions are often attended by bachelor or postgraduate students who observe, join in, support individuals, accompany, plan and teach parts of the class and discuss and reflect on the sessions. Didactical and methodical considerations are taken from Elemental Music and Dance Pedagogy (Carl Orff / Gunild Keetman) and Dance Dynamics (Wolfgang Stange). Within this resource-oriented approach, didactic reduction and extension play an important role. The aim of the sessions is to provide experiences and activities to further individual perception, expression and skills in music and movement as well as social learning and communication, and to develop the resources of each participant. Different types of instruments are made available to match the motor abilities and cognitive development of the participants. The wide range of activities includes exploration with instruments, voice and movement, greeting rituals, vocal and physical warm-up, playing with sound objects and materials, sound games, stories with music, listening, movement improvisation with and without materials, songs, accompaniments and improvisation. While working within a shared topic, different forms of cooperation are offered as well as individualized tasks so that each participant can play and learn at their own level while contributing to the whole.

**Markus Detterbeck (Helbling Verlagsgesellschaft m.b.H.)**

## From Action to Knowledge. Music Teaching: Creative and Logically Structured

How can we gradually develop and reinforce our pupils' musical abilities?
How can we integrate the principles of a structured musical education into our teaching in a way that is both sensible and enjoyable?
How can we get across supposedly 'unwieldy' topics such as the theory of music, contextual work and the history of music in ways that are effective and practically relevant?
Discover with the aid of materials that have proved their worth in practice how music teaching can apply new ideas and be oriented towards practice: a logical sequence of learning steps leads to the development and reinforcement of your pupils' musical abilities.
The models presented range from stimulating start-ups through rhythm games to cognitive contents (portraits of composers, the study of instruments...), but in every case have been developed from actual practice. The areas of music making, singing, listening and dancing are dealt with in ways that are both integrative and attractive to your pupils.
In addition, there are tips and suggestions as to how you can profitably integrate the new media into your teaching.
You will gain insight into:

- stimulating start-ups and rhythm games,
- materials and tips for vocal and instrumental music-making in class groups,
- a variety of innovative suggestions for your teaching that will give you and your pupils new and systematic access to music, providing many useful options for practice and for taking pleasure in own musical activities,
- new approaches to cognitive content: portraits of composers, the study of instruments, musical form etc.,
- tips and suggestions as to how you can profitably integrate the new media into your teaching,
- tips on methods you can use in your teaching.

**Teryl Dobbs / Elizabeth Hagedorn (University of Wisconsin-Madison)**

## Cultural Relevance and the Singing Voice: An Ad/Venture in Re/Imagining Music Learning and Teaching

In 2006 the University of Wisconsin-Madison's music education faculty recognized that its undergraduate curriculum was not meeting the needs of its future music educators. Specifically, the curriculum did not adequately prepare the students to successfully engage with increasingly diverse student populations. As a result, the faculty revised the music education curriculum over the next nine years, successfully rolling out a revamped undergraduate degree and teacher licensure program. At the core of the curriculum was the entwining of culturally relevant pedagogy (Ladson-Billings, 2009) with active music-making in a rapidly diversifying 21st century society. Pragmatically, the faculty understood that community musical partners were imperative to the revised program's success and that of its students, particularly in gaining a deeper understanding of multiple forms of music-making. Turning to diverse cultural networks present in Madison, Wisconsin, the faculty engaged with local cultural resources to craft musically rigorous and active learning experiences across a multicultural spectrum, both inside and outside the classroom. An exemplar of the revised curriculum emerged: a new course, *Teaching Vocal Styles in the Classroom.* Applying *Teaching Vocal Styles in the Classroom* as a window into the theoretical and practical foundations of curricular change, the presenters will elaborate how course experiences aided students to develop deeper understandings of multiple forms of music and how community partners were engaged as presenters in their field of expertise to facilitate students' exploring/experiencing facets of a particular music culture. As the first professor to teach the course, Elizabeth Hagedorn will share specific challenges and successes, especially those related to perforating the walls of the traditional classroom and engaging with culturally relevant teaching and transmission strategies. Teryl Dobbs, associate professor and chair of music education, will discuss the impetus for curricular revision and detail the theoretical foundations that drove the process.

Natassa Economidou-Stavrou (University of Nicosia) / Nopi Nicolaou Telemachou (University of Cyprus)

## Hitting a Tube: Music Synergies amongst University and High School Students

Nowadays, boomwhackers are widely used in music education contexts as an alternative tool to traditional classroom instruments, aiming at engaging students in challenging, non-conventional and sometimes spectacular music performances.

The aim of the current project was to introduce boomwhackers to a group of ten undergraduate Music Majors. Their task was to select three musical pieces/songs, make arrangements for a boomwhacker orchestra and perform them, as a flash mob, at the university cafeteria. Furthermore, students were asked to practice and perform these pieces additionally in a different context with high school students, in a joint musical performance.

Over a four-week-period informal learning practices, collaborative and active learning were applied in both educational contexts. A 90-minute workshop was organized for the secondary school students in their school by the university students, the researchers and the school music teacher, followed by a half an hour rehearsal. The workshop/rehearsal aimed at developing all the participants' ability of working and communicating musically as one group, leading to a joint ten minute performance in their school the same day.

The research involved a multiple-method approach including non-participant observations, field-notes, videotaping and semi-structured interviews at the beginning and end of the collaboration period.

Through this joint venture all parties benefited from various perspectives. The secondary school students were thrilled because they participated in a very challenging musical performance together with more advanced musicians, with whom they collaborated and worked together, using instruments they had never seen before. The university students had the opportunity to experience first-hand, both as students and as teachers, the benefits and the challenges of important approaches and methods they had got acquainted with in their music education course. Most importantly, the communication between the participants, their interaction and all the emotions they shared in rehearsal and during the performance, formed experiences not to be forgotten.

Paulo Esteireiro (NOVA University, Lisbon) / Carlos Gonçalves (INET-md Institute of Ethnomusicology)

## The Development of an Artistic Education Network with Students from Extracurricular Activities: Ten Years of the Project Artistic Season (2006–2016)

The Department of Arts and Multimedia Education (Madeira, Portugal) is a regional public authority which has a strong focus on networking. In 2005, this Governmental Department concluded that the annual volume of concerts performed by students in extracurricular activities lacked a systematic and networking approach, due to the huge demand of local and regional institutions. Thus, in 2006, the "Artistic Season" project was created. The project makes it possible to carry out an average of 200 performances per year, in cooperation with the municipalities of the Autonomous Region of Madeira and about 100 public and private entities in a decentralized perspective. Events are performed by about 20 artistic groups, comprising approximately 400 children and young students who partake in extracurricular activities. After ten years of activities, it is possible to conclude that this regional network of concerts allowed the development of a partnership model where entities were engaged from different areas, such as: media, tourism, city councils, schools, local and regional authorities, and other public and private entities. Currently, the main benefits of this concert network include:

(1) streamlining the concert halls of municipalities with fewer costs for local authorities;
(2) offering mostly free events to the population of the municipalities of the Autonomous Region of Madeira in various artistic areas – theater, music and dance;
(3) improvement of regional cultural offers available to tourism;
(4) improvement of students' motivation in extracurricular activities, providing them with frequent opportunities to perform in public professional production environments;
(5) encouraging the teachers to practice music outside the classroom context, allowing them to stay active not only as teachers but also as performers;
(6) improving the internal response process to requests for performances by public and private entities through annual planning.

Athina Fytika / Elesa Papakosta-Smyri (Ionian University, Corfu)

## Drawing Compositions: Introducing Contemporary Art to Kindergarten-Children through Piano-Experimentation

Kindergarten curricula typically incorporate both painting and music lessons as ideal vehicles for children's exploration of their visual and audio environment. The similarities of learning outcomes in both music and art design are striking. Pattern repetition, variety of expressive means, contrast, balance, form, and unity of work apply to both arts; hence these two teaching art areas are ideal for a unified and collaborative approach in terms of lesson planning. In January and February 2017 the 'Piano Pedagogy Program' of the Department of Music Studies of Ionian University in Greece organizes a targeted pedagogical approach to integrate contemporary art themes with piano improvisations and compositions for small groups of kindergarten-students (two to four). Three different art movements will be introduced: pointillism, cubism and pop art. The visual stimuli of each style will lead to a range of sonic explorations on the piano based on similar concepts in terms of patterns, contrasts, spatial placement and so forth. Graphic music notations of the improvisations produced will enable children to identify structural form and balance in music compositions. Moreover, graphic scores being the visual representations of sound will reinforce the art movement characteristics. Each lesson will be videotaped, observed and analyzed in order to evaluate the children's perception and comprehension of contemporary art and music. The aim of this pedagogical approach is to explore the use of a range of techniques, materials and vocabulary in order to enable children to develop their art and music skills. This interdependent teaching approach is expected to enhance certain skills that are essential for this developmental stage: concentration, visual and audio perception, sequencing, gross and fine motor development among others. Finally, piano teachers that are experimenting with preschool keyboard instruction will have the opportunity to assess the suitability of such interdisciplinary approaches.

Stacey Garrepy (University of North Carolina, Greensboro)

## 'Musicking Together': A Practical Theory of Change for Music and Special Education

Music educators' role in their schools involves service to the entire diverse cohort of students, including students with disabilities. Unfortunately, many music educators are insufficiently prepared to provide an inclusive space in their classroom for children with disabilities. As a result of this absence of preparation, many teachers focus primarily on the 'social' benefits of being in a general music class, rather than the participative value of 'musicking' as a part of the larger community. This lack of focus ultimately results in the denial of full access to the music curriculum for the student with disabilities. In this paper I will lay out a feasible theory of change with the ultimate goal of helping music teachers impact their learners, both those with or without special needs; as a result, both will gain full access to the music education curriculum and become fully immersed in 'musicking' as a community-based effort. I will first describe the ultimate goal of this model and its theoretical underpinnings in the works of Christopher Small; second, I will discuss the long-term visions/outcomes, which include educating teachers to work with children with disabilities, collaborating with both special education and music education, and teaching students to 'musick' as part of a larger community. Finally, I will discuss the preconditions necessary to produce these outcomes, focusing on strategies that are plausible, feasible, and measurable.

Julia Getino / Assumpta Valls / Cristina González-Martín (Universitat Autònoma de Barcelona)

## Pupils and Composers: From Listening to Contemporary Music to Musical Creation in the Classroom

"The composer in the classroom" is a project in which contemporary music and music creation converge in the primary school classroom through the presence of a professional composer. This project is part of a research study that intends to measure the effects of this cooperative work between students and music creators. Numerous studies have shown the benefits of music improvisation and composition as well as the use of contemporary music in primary classrooms. In addition, other research work has found several advantages stemming from the contact between children and composers in a formal classroom setting. This project was carried out in five schools located in Barcelona (Spain), and involved three composers: Agustí Charles (1960), Ramon Humet (1968) and Bernat Vivancos (1973). In our presentation, we will first describe the design and implementation of this project, and subsequently discuss some early findings based on one of the participant teacher's testimony. The most relevant stages of this project are the following:

- listening to and analysis of a contemporary composer's piece,
- creation of a music composition that incorporates some of the resources and compositional elements studied in the previous stage,
- the composer's visit to the classroom in order to work collaboratively with the students on their musical piece,
- modifications of the students' composition taking into account the composer's suggestions,
- a final concert with all the schools involved in the project.

In conclusion, evidence suggests that "The Composer in the Classroom" is an innovative and useful approach that has a very positive effect on primary school students. We will argue that the interaction between composers and these students seems to lead to a rich and complete music-learning experience through the exercise of musical creation.

**Rûta Girdzijauskiene / Emilija Sakadolskienė / Sandra Rimkutė-Jankuvienė (Klaipeda University)**

## Network for Music Education: Lithuanian Case Study

The origins of the systems of music education in Lithuania lie in the 14th century. The earliest documentation of the Vilnius Cathedral School in 1397 accounts of boys learning ecclesiastical chant and receiving musical training to sing in church choirs and become music teachers (Jareckaitė, 2006). Over the following 600 years, education experienced significant transformations until the contours of the contemporary system of music education were established in the 1960s. The Soviet school of the 1990s consisted of an authoritarian regime and one-sided educational content. The focus on results faced a resolute change in 1990 when Lithuania regained its independence (Girdzijauskienė & Sakadolskienė, 2016). In reaction to the Soviet concept of education, the network of institutions related to and responsible for music education was initiated. The institutions attached directly to the Ministries of Education and Culture, associations of music teachers and musicians, publishing houses and various independent organizations. However, despite an abundant and diverse number of institutions involved with music education, there is still a lack of purpose and an incompatibility of activities, when it comes to a unified vision of music education. The aim of this report is to present a model for the network of institutions related to music education by assessing the type and strength of synergy among its individual components, by providing the trends and potentials for intensified cooperation. For this purpose ten institutions were selected and their performance was expertly assessed. Assessment in this case can be understood as a qualitative evaluation under research performed by Lithuanian music pedagogy experts. Five specialist representatives from different institutions were chosen, namely the Ministry of Education and Science, Lithuanian Academy of Music and Theatre, Association of Music Teachers, Education Development Centre and Ministry of Culture. Referring to the obtained data, the most significant amendments included: formation of music education policy, preparation of the programs of music teaching, teacher support and their ongoing training, and scholarly and methodological publications. It appeared that the issues related to music education policy were most effectively addressed in the institutions affiliated with the Ministry of Education and Science. However, the Association of Music Teachers and high schools preparing music teachers and promoting the science of music pedagogy have the greatest impact on music education in Lithuania.

**Bernhard Gritsch / Magdalena Steinmayr (University of Music and Performing Arts Graz)**

## "B9 – Beethoven for All"

The Institute of Music Education at the University of Music and Performing Arts Graz (Austria) has taken an innovative and forward-looking approach in the education of future music teachers. By including a constantly evolving music education project in its education program, the institute encouraged its students to take on larger roles in the music education sector and to integrate diversified cultural activities, institutions and their members into their future teaching practice: "Working on the project has taken away my fears about handling projects like these by myself." As part of the musical initiative "B9 – Beethoven for all", the students involved were given the opportunity to experience different artists and teachers but especially themselves as an important and multiplying part of our cultural life. Together with more than 150 pupils, they developed different forms of onstage action (e.g. elements of dance, singing, theatre and rap) to Beethoven's Ninth Symphony over a period lasting more than five months. Supported by an outstanding, personal cooperation between mentors from six secondary schools, professors from the institute, experts from Opera Graz and the Philharmonic Orchestra Graz, results of their work were finally presented on two occasions on the opera stage in April 2016. The institute demonstrates a high motivation and commitment to sharing the multifaceted knowledge gained through "B9", verifying its sustainability and allowing more teachers or institutions to be inspired by or replicate parts of the project: Initiating a diploma thesis about "B9" – based on the principles of ethnography and the participant observer technique an involved student gathered, described and analysed as many processes as possible, completing her thesis with transcribed group discussions and interviews. A 15-minute professional film documentary recording students' progress during "B9" was broadcast across Austria on ORF III in July 2016. Meanwhile, the film documentary is available with English subtitles. Furthermore articles and reports in various conferences have contributed to the dissemination of our ideas.

**Hubert Gruber / Josef Buchner (University College of Teacher Education, Baden bei Wien)**

## How to Create Inverted Classroom Videos for Teaching and Learning Music in and out of the Classroom

The project "How to Create Inverted Classroom Videos" is a joint venture between Hubert Gruber and Josef Buchner. The former is a music teacher and educationalist and the latter an e-learning and blended-learning specialist, working at the same university. In September 2015 they started their 'joint adventure' in collaboration with their students. At first, learning sequences with music were developed, for example how to compose short melodies by combining short stories with the names of the notes. Another learning sequence demonstrated how to create a rhythm and melody by walking on the syllables of words in a sentence. The third sequence showed how to learn the words, rhythm and melody of a song. Finally the university students were instructed how to put such video-sequences together to make their own inverted Classroom videos for their school pupils. How to create such videos can also be learned in advanced teacher training courses. In the workshop, Hubert Gruber and Josef Buchner will show examples of their collaboration by using parts of the videos "How to compose a melody", "How to develop a Sound Word Path" and "How to learn to sing a song with an inverted classroom video". They will detail how to create them, how to work with them and how to use them for research in practice and theory. There will be the opportunity to experiment with the videos.

**Anette Hamelink / Adrie Gloudemans (Kunstbedrijf Arnhem)**

## Incredibox and Spoken Word: The Combination of Dutch Language Lessons, Music Lessons and Digital Media in Primary Schools in Arnhem, the Netherlands

Adrie Gloudemans, digital media teacher (Kunstbedrijf Arnhem), Annette Hamelink, music teacher (Kunstbedrijf Arnhem), and primary schools in Arnhem (Het Klinket De Sterrenkring Kunstrijk De Vaart) cooperate in this project. Our aim is to show primary school teachers how to work creatively with digital tools. Moreover, we wanted to clarify how to integrate the arts with the regular curriculum, such as mathematics and languages. Children come into contact with music everywhere. Many children also love to be actively engaged in music: to sing, move or play. These observations support our theory that music is more than pleasure; there is scientific evidence that musical activities have positive effects on the development of children, for instance in areas such as language, social and emotional skills, motor skills, creativity, and the ability to concentrate. The principles of trial and error, of exploring and learning with the teacher as a coach determine our decisions from a pedagogical perspective. The students discuss their experience of music: for example, where and when they listen to music. Subsequently, they write a story about this topic. Using that story, the students explore the rhythm of the language, while presenting the story. An artist visits the classroom and gives a performance, demonstrating different ways in which language and music can be combined. The students work with www.incredibox.com to create different beats that can be incorporated in their stories. Finally, they make a spoken word piece about listening to music and they present this to their parents.

**Warren Haston (The University of Hartford's Hartt School)**

## A Joint Extracurricular Musical Venture between an Elementary School and a Private University

The purpose of this practice-based paper was to describe the mutual benefits, as well as challenges, of a partnership between a higher education school of music and a local elementary magnet school that serves underprivileged students from an urban area. Music teacher preparation programs may play an integral role in ensuring continued access to quality instrumental music instruction for some marginalized students. Students attending the magnet school are brought to this school from a multitude of communities in and around a major metropolitan area through a state program designed to alleviate the segregation and fiscal boundaries often found in the area schools. Although elementary general music instruction taught by highly qualified music teachers is compulsory for students, the school offers limited, elective instrumental music study. In order to provide extracurricular instrumental music instruction, a partnership was created with a local university responsible for preparing future music educators. Undergraduate music education majors in their junior year are required to take two instrumental methods/pedagogy courses (winds, percussion, and strings). Over the course of one academic year, undergraduates teach three hours a week for twenty weeks in an authentic learning context that may improve music teacher identity development, career commitment, and understanding of the intricacies, challenges and rewards of teaching music. Two university faculty members observe and supervise the undergraduates while they teach. This supervision allows for assessment of the undergraduates' teaching as well as facilitates conversations during the instrumental methods courses held on the university campus. Additionally, graduate students mentor the undergraduates and are mentored themselves by the faculty. In order to make an economic difference and respond to social inclusion, students who are unable to pay the nominal registration fee can request financial assistance, which has been granted for every request.

**Emiel Heijnen / Melissa Bremmer (Amsterdam University of the Arts)**

## Performances, Social Interventions & Transformations: Interdisciplinary Arts Educational Design

Authentic arts education (Haanstra, 2001 and 2011) is a pedagogical approach which criticizes the isolated and anachronistic nature of traditional arts education and its lack of connection to both contemporary, often interdisciplinary professional arts practice and to the needs of the student. Therefore, authentic arts education aims for meaningful connections between both the interests of the student and the professional world of the arts. Emile Heijnen (2015) has explored both the students' artistic activities and contemporary professional arts practices. His research has shown that students often participate in communities of practice that reflect popular culture, and that contemporary arts practice concentrates on conceptual, interdisciplinary and collaborative production. Authentic arts education draws on both these worlds when designing an arts curriculum. The paper gives an insight into a project carried out at Amsterdam University of the Arts. During their first year of a two-year course, students of the Master of Education in Arts collaborate in a course in which they learn how to design and execute an interdisciplinary arts programme based on the principles of authentic arts education. These students with backgrounds in music, dance, drama or visual arts education are free to implement their arts programme in primary, secondary or higher education. At the end of the master's course, students present the process and results of their interdisciplinary arts programme in the form of a short video documentary. This master's course aims at contributing to the development of a new generation of arts teachers who can operate in the field of contemporary, interdisciplinary arts education. The objective of this presentation is to give insight into the design of this innovative, interdisciplinary course, to discuss its underlying educational and artistic principles and to present documentaries that exemplify the work of the students.

**Fritz Höfer (Yamaha Music Europe GmbH.)**

## New Forms of Teaching and Learning in Piano Teaching Thanks to the Integration of Digital Techniques: Yamaha Discpiano Enspire and Yamaha TransAcoustics

Technology, media and musical instrument building have always influenced musical production and reception. Works of music composed for the piano have naturally always been determined by the respective tonal and technical possibilities of the instrument. While the development of traditional orchestral instruments seems to a large extent completed with the Romantic period, the 20th and 21st century have brought about extensive paradigmatic changes in the area of electronic musical instruments. Therefore a profound distinction between analogous and digital, respectively electronic instruments, based on computer-technology, can be observed nowadays. Most experts in classical music prefer analogous instruments and refer to electronic digital instruments as 'false', 'unnatural' or 'artificial'. However, would it not be a logic consequence to apply these attributes to any instrument with the exception of the human voice? Should they not be referred to as technical equipment with a more or less intensive connection with the human body? Yamaha has a long tradition in the production analogous instruments as well as in the development and production of electronic instruments. For several decades there have been attempts of this world wide enterprise to combine an analogous and electronic tradition of piano building. Present results are Yamaha Dicpinao Enspire and the Transacoustic series respectively technique. These instruments offer the following innovations:

- acoustic instruments with alternating possibilities of electronic sound production,
- automatic performance on an acoustic piano (Optical sensors register finest nuances of the actual performance of a player on the keyboard and the pedals – including half-pedaling and make it possible to record and recall all these pieces of acoustic information. The keys move as though touched by a magic hand recalling what has been recorded in full detail.),
- electronic samples that are not recalled over loudspeakers but via the sound chest,
- ways of recording and recalling one's own play with electronic or natural sounds,
- access to a data base storing recordings on the instrument that can be recalled via the keyboard,
- USB/MIDI-interface to establish a connection to a PC/tablet and make use of respective software,
- App control.

All these achievements result in new didactical and methodological challenges for piano teaching. Based on the assumption that not only musical production and reception but also instrumental didactics are profoundly influenced by these developments I will refer to innovative ways of learning and teaching inspired by the possibilities of these new instruments.

**Angelika Holzer (University College of Teacher Education Styria, Graz)**

## Dance ALL together! Students and Children with Special Needs Dance together

A dance project bringing together children with special needs and students will be presented. The students are studying to become special educational needs (SEN) teachers at the University College of Teacher Education in Styria (Austria). The children and staff from the School for Children with Special Needs (Kalvarienbergstraße, Graz) strove to create an inclusive learning environment. By combining these two institutions, a mutually beneficial environment was achieved. The main objective was to incorporate practical lessons and theoretical knowledge to create a lasting and applicable learning experience for the SEN students. The dance project began in 2012. Since there are not many opportunities for children with special needs to get engaged in artistic activities, the director of the school was very interested in the project and the teachers and other staff members welcomed the participants warmly. Until now, the project has been carried out with 112 SEN students. Twelve to seventeen SEN students and ten to twenty children with different special needs from several classes work together. Each group of SEN students attend the school six times and dance in 75-minute-sessions with the same group of children. I have always been in charge of these classes. Basic principles and methods (secure surroundings, a focus on competences, common denominators, free choices, improvisation, a shared theme ...) obviously support an inclusive environment where everybody is able to join in. All SEN students declared that this was an exceptional experience. The children appreciated the opportunity to get in contact with other children and the chance to communicate through their prime capabilities. The project showed that encountering people with severe disabilities helped the students to overcome their anxieties about interacting with the children and allowed them to get involved with them.

**Maria Honsig (Salzburg) / Maria Majno (Milano)**

## European Mozart Ways

The European Mozart Ways (EMW) is an international network connecting cities, regions and institutions in ten European countries visited by Mozart. Mozart travelled more than half of his life – from London to Naples, from Paris to Bratislava. This was essential in shaping the personal and artistic development of this great figure in European culture. Mozart left his footprints throughout around 200 places – in today's Austria, Belgium, the Czech Republic, France, Germany, Great Britain, Italy, the Netherlands, Slovakia and Switzerland. These ideas inspired the following project: Cities and regions, cultural and touristic organizations, and academic institutions are represented in the Association "European Mozart Ways" (EMW), founded in 2002 during the lead-up to the Europe-wide celebrations for the 250$^{th}$ anniversary of Mozart's birth, as an initiative of the Province of Salzburg.
Mozart's journeys serve as a model for routes intended to stimulate sustainable cultural tourism in the relevant regions, and as a basis for cross-border cooperation of members in artistic, cultural, educational and scientific projects. As a result, the Mozart itineraries have been nominated a "Major Cultural Route" by the Council of Europe in 2004, and represent the only instance centered on the life and work of a musician.
Several educational projects have been developed in this context:

- "Moving With Mozart" / exchanges in concerts, choir performances, awards
- "There is More to Mozart" / videos, film-experiments
- "Mozart Stories" / storytelling
- "Let's Talk Mozart" / language & music beyond borders
- "Mozart Classes" / school and classroom initiatives.

**Clara Horbach (University of Music and Performing Arts Munich)**

## Music and Movement with Unaccompanied Refugee Minors

At the Münchner Waisenhaus (Munich Orphanage) unaccompanied refugee minors of all ages are housed. In cooperation with the University of Music I started a music and movement project with a group of them (aged 15 to 18) in December 2015. Most of them come from Afghanistan and are already able to speak German. In the beginning there were about eight participants but after a few weeks we had a core group of four to five youths. For the rest of the school year the lessons took place once a week in the big hall of the orphanage in Munich. Initially I wanted to focus on rhythm. We worked on easy rhythmical patterns beginning with imitation and then progressing to improvising and inventing our own patterns. Through imitation, the youths learned body percussion sequences supported by simple movement patterns that were then transferred to cajons and other instruments. Structured as ABA-forms or rounds we soon were able to play these sequences polyphonically. Rhythmic reaction games accompanied by piano or vocal improvisation trained musical understanding and helped build musical ideas. In addition, I later taught easy songs from different cultures according to the "Music Learning Theory" by Edwin Gordon. Besides considering rhythmic aspects I put another focus on movement. Each lesson started with a physical warm up to prepare the youths for activities with body and voice. I considered posture and body language of particular importance to improve their body sensation. Then we started with free movement in space to help the youths connect with their bodies. After a while I introduced simple choreographies but also encouraged the youths to incorporate their own ideas. In terms of a methodic-didactic approach Edwin Gordon's "Music Learning Theory", Rudolf von Laban's approach to movement in education and the experiences I made during the "AOSA Orff Levels" influenced my decisions. My intentions were to enhance self competence, social skills, intercultural competence, practical competence in music and movement, artistic competences and cognitive competence in music and movement. Because of the specific target group, goals like orientation and safety, group identification, openness, respect and integration were of great importance.

Gabriel Imthurn (University of Applied Sciences and Arts Northwestern Switzerland FHNW)

## "Basis Check Voice": A Diagnosis Tool

"Basic Check Voice" provides information about the student's vocal condition. It serves as a diagnostic tool to improve teaching preparation and to provide individualized feedback from teacher to student. It is intended for lower secondary school when the vocal change takes place and singing skills have to be re-established physically and mentally. The student first records his spoken voice and then sings a song three times: together with a singer, only with piano accompaniment and lastly with a rhythm pattern. Afterwards the assessment sheet is filled out by the teacher. The theoretical background has different origins. Hoene and Thurmann (2011) emphasize the importance of diagnosis in music teaching in heterogeneous classes. In our first explorative study, pupils had to send a recorded song to find out what teaching methods and which content suited best. The encouraging results led to the idea of "Basic Check Voice". Hasselhorn (2015) has validated a competency model for musical skills. The six levels of vocal skills in his model provide the only validated part of the first version of the new check. Fuchs (2015) emphasizes the importance of teachers observing young voices. A couple of ideas in the check were taken from his recommendations. Overall, "Basic Check Voice" is a typical "Assessment for Learning" tool. The first version of the check currently is in a trial phase. More than 100 pupils and students have recorded their tests. Singers and teachers fill out the assessment sheet for each test person. By comparing the results, it becomes clear which parameters of the test can be validly assessed. It is the goal to create a handy tool for music teachers, which helps to create a basis for individual feedback and the preparation of singing lessons.

Rûta Kanteruka

## Teaching Music in the Differentiated Classroom

*A different way to learn is what the kids are calling for... All of them are talking about how our one-size-fits-all delivery system – which mandates that everyone learn the same thing at the same time, no matter what their individual needs – has failed them.* (Seymour Sarason).

Teachers can differentiate the content, the process and the product according to students' readiness / development, interest and learning style.

Differentiating content (knowledge, skills and attitudes we want students to learn) requires that students are pre-tested so the teacher can identify the students who do not require direct instruction. Differentiating the process requires varying learning activities and strategies to provide appropriate methods for students to explore the concepts. It is important to give students alternative paths to manipulate the ideas embedded within the concept (different grouping methods, graphic organizers, maps, diagrams, or charts). When differentiating the product, we vary the complexity of the product that students create to demonstrate mastery of the concepts; students below grade level may have different performance expectations than students above grade level (i.e. more complex or more advanced thinking).

As mentioned before, we also need to be aware of students' readiness, interest and learning style. Some students are ready for different concepts, skills, or strategies; others may lack the foundation needed to progress to further levels. Students' interest inventories provide information to plan different activities that respond to the individual student's interest.

Individual student preference concerning the question of where, when or how students obtain and process information (visual, auditory, kinesthetic; multiple intelligences; environment, social organization, physical circumstance, emotional climate, psychological climate) is also an important aspect of a successful experience of differentiation.

In this Good Practice/Educational Experience Paper (PPT) good examples of differentiating music lessons will be presented.

**Eva Koeniger (Music School Vienna)**

## Klasse musizieren! Insights into the Project "ELEMU" in Viennese Primary Schools

"ELEMU" is a cooperate project between Viennese Music Schools and the Viennese school board which was launched in the 2013/14. "ELEMU" is an abbreviation of "Elemental Music" in the narrower and broader sense. The main focus is making music together in regular primary school classes. Our focus is on children aged six to ten years. The primary school curriculum demands one music lesson per week; ELEMU-classes receive an extra music lesson. Both lessons take place within the frame of compulsory schooling under the guidance of both the music school expert (lecturer from an official Viennese music school) and the school teacher in the form of team teaching. The core of "ELEMU" is the active making of music involving the entire class. "ELEMU" is free of charge for parents. The School of Music Vienna, in collaboration with the Music and Art University of Vienna and the Johann Sebastian Bach Music School are currently supporting 24 primary schools. Almost all of these schools have completed a four year cycle, which means there is an ELEMU-class at each level. In addition the Viennese Board of Education has introduced "ELEMU" to 13 extra locations. In this way 2.650 primary school children from 37 schools in 106 classes will benefit from "ELEMU". Working with the basic principle of "making music together" the teaching content and emphasis varies according to the artistic experience of the music teacher. The focal point for each location is one based either on singing, percussion, music theatre, dance, string or brass instruments, band projects, world music or folk – the possibilities are endless and always adaptable to the locations, circumstances and needs. The participation of the children in this process does not require any pre-knowledge or education. Each individual in a class can contribute from the very beginning towards making music together with his/her own skill and experience. "ELEMU" fulfills many needs and offers an inclusive and diverse opportunity, irrelevant of ethnicity, family background or individual history. Integration, mutual understanding and esteem naturally flourish in such an atmosphere and children find their own sentient value of music and development potential.

**Wolfgang Kosmata (Falco Private Foundation, Vienna) / Rob Bolland**

## "Helden von heute – Falco Goes School"

After the death of Falco, his mother Maria Hölzel founded the "Falco Private Foundation" in 2004 together with his friend and sponsor Ronald Seunig. The main task of the foundation was primarily the financial security and medical care of Falco's mother, who was seriously ill. In April 2014 Mrs. Hölzel died and the current foundation mission, defined as "the preservation of the artistic heritage" and the "fostering of Austrian young artists", became effective. Subsequently, the foundation produced a catalog with proposals for the implementation of these tasks. The management board decided on the promotional concept and talent competition "Helden von heute (Heroes of Today) – Falco goes school". "Helden von heute" is one of Falco's song titles. The song from the 1980s is of immediate interest today, ending in the refrain with an expression of hopeful confidence: "Everyone is waiting, everyone is waiting for the HEROES OF TODAY". The project "Falco goes school" encourages talents to be forwarded and supported as early as possible. Now, after the introduction of whole-day schools (Ganztagsschulen) in Austria, there is an increasing number of school-initiated music and singing projects (singing, instrumental lessons, songwriting, bands, music programming) which often reveal the musical talents of the Austrian pupils. On February 19th 2016, the "Falco Private Foundation" started the competition and invited school initiatives and the resulting talents to promote their music and vocal performances on the Talents Page www.falcogoesschool.at. A total of 100 music videos were registered for the competition – 95 for pop music and five for classical music. A four-week 'public voting' should give the advisors, who had to act as jurors on the basis of the charter certificate, a clear idea of the 'public opinion'. The executive board of the foundation provided a funding budget of EUR 45.000. The amount of the grant was allocated in equal parts of EUR 15.000, to the top ranked projects in three categories. In order to offer the "TOP 15 talents" the opportunity to show their skills in a live performance, "Falco Goes School Summer Show" was organized in July. Furthermore ten talented students were given an opportunity to work on their own compositions and cover versions, which will be released in February 2017, with their teachers and supported by the producer Rob Bolland. The project was received very positively and the website www.falcogoesschool.at has already attracted more than 2.4 million visitors.

Judita Kučerová (Masaryk University, Brno)

## Folk Song in Czech Schools: A Challenge for Music Education and Ethnomusicology?

Folk song is traditionally the starting point of music education in Czech schools. The author presents her view on perspectives of musical folklore heritage under the conditions of contemporary cultural and social developments. Based on findings of music-education and ethnomusicological research, the author illustrates possibilities of cooperation between both scientific disciplines. On the basis of specific examples from school practice, this paper demonstrates possible applications of the results of ethnomusicological research into school environments. Folk music and folk song are means and goals not only for musical activities, but they can also be effectively integrated into different areas of education. The paper is focused on interdisciplinary approaches within scientific disciplines and the chances of their integration in the school curriculum.

Kenneth Liske (University of Wisconsin Oshkosh)

## "Arts-Integrated Instruction": Curricular Innovation for Pre-Service Educators and University-School-Community Partnerships

"Arts-integrated instruction" as a pedagogical approach is characterized by the congruent connection of a creative art form with other subject contents in a manner that enhances learning outcomes in both areas. This is differentiated from arts-enhanced, arts-infused, or arts-centric instruction, which may capitalize on research-based learning enhancements derived from music and the arts in a supportive role, but without purposeful objectives for artistic growth. The "Kennedy Center Model" for arts-integrated instruction provides a framework and definition for this teaching approach at any grade level, however, to be effective, it requires teachers to have skill, knowledge, and pedagogical understanding both in an art form and other content areas. A primary way to enable this is through formation of school-based interdisciplinary collaborative teacher teams that include arts specialists. Drawing upon the expertise of each teacher, this encourages true integration: children sharing creative classroom experiences, and teachers creating new and evolving strategies to meet discrete objectives together. "ArtsCore" is a grant-funded program at the University of Wisconsin Oshkosh that fosters wide-ranging initiatives to promulgate the understanding and best practice of arts-integrated instruction, including curricular innovation in teacher education and professional development, intra-university collaboration, and university-school-community partnerships. The paper broadly describes implementation of the "ArtsCore" program itself, with detail on pre-service preparation for arts-integrated instruction. This entails the curricular re-design and co-teaching of methods courses in elementary, early-childhood, special education, music, and art education to include base knowledge and skill, and to enable collaboration among teacher candidates in those areas. This also includes the development of external student internships and a "teacher in residency" program, placing student teachers in schools with existing interdisciplinary teacher teams. These innovations intend to give future teachers greater readiness to effectively implement arts-integrated instruction, with the potential of expanding the approach throughout many schools in the region.

Vedrana Markovic (Music Academy, Cetinje)

## Initial Solfeggio Teaching with Visually Impaired Students in Montenegro: Examples of Openness and Cooperation with the "Resource Centre for Children and Youth in Podgorica"

The "Resource Centre for Children and Youth in Podgorica" is the only specialized institution in Montenegro for the education of students with visual impairment. Even though there are a certain number of young people with striking music abilities, they face numerous difficulties on their path to receiving a professional music education. In our efforts to make this path easier, an initial solfeggio teaching program was launched in the resource center in the academic year 2010/11, following a 2009 study on the music abilities of resource center students. This program is a product of cooperation between professors from the Music Academy Cetinje and special education experts working at the resource center. This program has been successfully implemented by a music-education teacher at the aforementioned center, a former Cetinje Academy student with visual impairment. The goal of the program is that students become music literate in Braille music code and that they acquire initial solfeggio knowledge to be able to participate in the learning process of music schools. We have conceived methods and a pedagogical approach in accordance with the nature of the visual disability, with the intention of enabling the program participants to acquire knowledge faster and more easily. The author of this work presented the methodological solutions in a doctoral thesis *Development of the Initial Solfeggio Teaching Model in Working with Blind and Partially Sighted Children*. In the framework of this program, 45 minutes classes are organized twice a week, in accordance with the program of the solfeggio course taught in music schools. Participants who complete the initial solfeggio program successfully are more easily integrated in regular classes in music schools. Being music literate means they are able to independently follow the solfeggio and instrumental classes and to participate in all activities of the music school. A larger number of blind and partially sighted children and students in music schools show that they can successfully receive a music education, but there needs to be greater support from both music educators and society as a whole.

**Irena Müller-Brozovic (University of Arts Berne)**

## Different Perspectives of People Involved in a Participative Project. Report and Reflection on a Project Realized by a 5th-Grade Class, the Basel Symphony Orchestra and Media Artists

The "Basel Department of Culture" supports cooperative projects of cultural institutions and schools. In the presented project a music mediator, three musicians from the orchestra, three teachers, two media artists and a class of 11-year-old children over a five months open process create a sound response to a work played by the orchestra. The young performers move, sing and play traditional instruments as well as new ones (e.g. hair dryers on bottles) combined with new media such as light and Wii-sensors. The performance takes place on stage during two concerts of the Basel Symphony Orchestra. The project observes the different experiences, reflects on them considering the perspectives of the participants. In this context various goals are focused on: artistic, pedagogical, strategic and social aims, such as an authentic artistic performance, an intense and conscious perception, an openness and respect for others (people, music and media), ways of coping with problems and irritations, self-efficacy, empowerment, connections with the curriculum, aspects of change management, openness to new audiences and social realities. The approach is explorative and starts with questions and challenges derived from the orchestral piece – a musical homage to Basel. The different members of the team lead a workshop group each, and choose different starting points. The groups present their results at the end of each workshop. This collection forms the material for the piece which is 'built' in co-construction. The deconstruction and aesthetic transformation of musical ideas led to a new piece of music with high relevance to the children. Different grades of participation, functions and qualities of cultural mediation, and the theory of aesthetic transformation and how it relates to performance are reflected on. Obviously cooperation projects need the consent of the school director, the artistic director and management. All people involved must communicate clearly and declare their role in the project. The teacher has to deal with the different perspectives. His attitude and communication within the project is essential to its success.

**Lina Oravec (University of Koblenz-Landau) / Julia Lutz (Folkwang University of Arts, Essen)**

## Learning from and with Each Other: Embedding Cooperation of In-Service Generalist and Pre-Service Specialist Music Teachers in University Music Teacher Training

In several European countries, most primary school music lessons are taught by generalist teachers with little or no musical training who consequently lack the confidence and skills to teach music. Research has shown that cooperation with music specialists among the teaching staff can increase this confidence (Hammel, 2011). In order to overcome the situation of non-specialist music teaching, one should make use of the opportunity to use the few music specialists as multipliers and facilitators for the colleagues in one's own school. Cooperative structures should be embedded within the music teacher training at university in order to familiarize music specialists with their new role serving not only the children, but also the non-specialist colleagues. Our presentation is about two similar projects that aim at initiating cooperation between pre-service music specialists and in-service generalist teachers. One project is centered at the University of Munich (since 2011), guided by Prof. Dr. Julia Lutz, the other at the University of Koblenz-Landau (since 2016), guided by Prof. Dr. Lina Oravec. Project evaluation shows that not only the generalists but also the pre-service specialist teachers benefit greatly from this cooperation.

Maria Papathanasiou (London / Thessaloniki)

## Music and Literature in Connection with Society: An Educational, Sociological and Humanistic Approach

In difficult times music can be a tool for students to shape life values and ethos, to awaken their awareness about social issues and to find balance and harmony between themselves, the others and the world. In ancient Greece, philosophers like Aristotle and Plato connected music education with ethos, harmony, justice and moral values, whereby young people can gain hope, faith and strength for a better world.

These ideas, still relevant nowadays, suggest a holistic approach to teaching music, considering the respective sociological and cultural background. The students' awareness is shaped by referring to the circumstances under which music was made: Was it inspired by a celebration, motivated by a revolution, connected with fear, hope, happiness, mourning, peace, war?

This approach can be greatly enhanced by establishing a connection between music and literature. Literary texts can create engaging images for the students and excite their imagination. But most importantly, literature can enhance their awareness about social issues, awaken empathy for others and help students identify themselves through the literary story as they feel sympathy for the hero, come closer and become more familiar with the circumstances.

In this paper, the theoretical background is presented first, by referring to approaches inspired by John Dewey, Jean Piaget, Maria Montessori and others and integrating methods of visual learning such as Neil Fleming's VAK/VARK model, interdisciplinary methods, ideas derived from the area of multicultural and multimedial learning, the Suzuki method and elements of the methods established by Carl Orff, Émile Jaques-Dalcroze and Zoltán Kodály. Practical examples provide an insight into projects connecting students with society through music and literature. Excerpts from novels were combined with music so as to: (1) provide stimuli for students to read how a foreigner found comfort and relief though music in a foreign place and introducing them to the middle-Eastern instrument "nei"; (2) help them realize how people were releasing their sufferings and regaining their faith and hope through the traditional Spanish custom of music "saeta"; and (3) raise their awareness for the fight for women's equality.

Milena Petrovic (Faculty of Music University of Arts, Belgrade)

## Integrating Multimedia Approaches into Music Performance with Music Education Students

A multiplicity of approaches is required to enlarge students' motivation and music understanding. The key component to arts education for today's students is variety (Sloboda, 2001). One of the most long-standing and effective extra-curricular arts activities is participation in musicals, referring to real life as one of its key attractions (Upitis, 2010). Introducing technologies and integrating possibilities of interactivity and multimedia are important components in music education nowadays and are used to develop new aspects in the musical performance (Rodrigues et al., 2005). Multimedia combines of text, sound, pictures, images, animation and video establish a rich scenic context for theatrical and musical action, exploring new forms of artistic expression. Students become inventive and motivated (Ward, 2009) and their musical abilities are enhanced through the use of ICT (Savage, 2007).

The main aim of our project is to increase music understanding, motivation, dedication and cooperation of music education students through the integration of multimedia in the musical performance.

The pedagogical approach implies 'crossing' music and performing arts with multimedia. It combines aspects of music, theatre, movement and multimedia and gravitates around a collection of visual, theatrical and musical actions. Music education students are included in the realization-process of making a musical.

Embodied learning is inherent in the performance of a musical, integrating experiences that engage the body, senses, emotions, imagination and intellect. The interdisciplinary nature of the musical encompasses all of the fine and performing arts, together with the use of multimedia.

The benefits are evident in the long run. Students learn to interact with one another, develop a deeper and sophisticated sense of creative identity and gain 'ownership' over the creative process and product.

Ilonka Pucihar (Music School Vrhnika, Academy of Music Ljubiljana)

## Music and Movement: An Indivisible Whole

We create music with our bodies; the language of music is sensual, reflecting lived experience. Both music-theoretical and technical-interpretative elements should be derived from lived and embodied musical experience based on the paradigm of embodied music cognition. Throughout the 2013/2014 school year, weekly 90-minute workshops were organised at the Vrhnika Music School to enable music teachers' experiences of movement to music that expand the awareness of the body, offer opportunities for teaching music with the inclusion of physical movement, and enhance well-being. Each meeting involved: (1) calming and preparing the body through relaxation, breathing, awareness of individual body parts, and contemplative movement; (2) integration of music and physical movement through kinaesthetic awareness of musical elements (tempo, rhythm, meter, pitch and melody, harmony, dynamics, agogics, articulation, phrasing) and the associated possibilities for teaching; (3) free enjoyment, the joy of group dance with simple choreography. A combination of somatic movement approaches were employed in conjunction with selected recorded classical or improvised music. Through observation and a questionnaire involving five regular participants – teachers of piano, flute, clarinet and music theory – links were investigated between their experience of the workshop and their well-being, their experience of music, their interpersonal relationships, and the transferability of their experiences to their pedagogical work. Positive correlations emerged between the experience at the workshops and general well-being, in particular with physical and mental relaxation; with the experience of music, which is more intense, freer and more fluid; and with interpersonal relationships, which are calmer and more authentic, empathetic and forgiving. In their work, the participants feel more creative, bolder and more confident. They also report gaining new ideas and being better able to express themselves and offer support.

Hans van Regenmortel (Musica, Impulse Centre for Music, Neerpelt)

## "UKELILA": An Artistic Catalyst for Musical Adventures in and outside Schools

The Genk (Belgium) based "Ukelila project" combines the emancipatory effects of a school orchestra with exploring new approaches to music education in primary schools by taking a radically aural and artistic stance. The project invites professional music teachers to explore new ways supporting children to become musically skilful on their instrument of choice. On a long term basis, "Ukelila" goes in search of collaboration between primary schools, music schools and local ensembles, aiming at an inclusive approach in a context of diversity, and with interesting mutual effects.
In this educational adventure the focus is on musicality rather than on music, the latter being the expectable outcome of the former. Teachers are coached and supported in the basic starting points of the project. They are expected to provide a context where 'making your own music together' is taken literally.
"Ukelila" questions the regular 'step-by-step' approach of 'first technique, then music' which is ordinarily and often uncritically applied. Rather, it opts for an integration of musical understanding and skills by taking an artistic stance from the very start.
Connections are made with local initiatives and ensembles that are eager to enthuse children to join them. These connections result in a win-win situation for all: regular school teachers start questioning their own views on musical and general development; children are able to take part in 'real musical life' in the community; amateur musicians are confronted with less common approaches and music; music teachers bring new insights into music schools.
This talk is about the opportunities and problems that arise when music teachers are being challenged by another paradigm for musical development, and how 'a broad artistic margin' in a networking context can help.

Fabian Rieser (Dr. Hoch's Konservatorium Frankfurt am Main)

## Attachment Theory as a Tool to Enhance Teacher Reflexivity

In Western classical instrumental learning, one-to-one tuition is still the predominant way of teacher-student interaction. This interaction mode is the result of its historical development stemming from the medieval master-apprentice model. However, young musicians nowadays face unprecedented challenges in their professional development. These rapid changes require constant adaptation and self-development on part of the students.

Conversely, these changes also affect the teacher's role when acting in the studio. It is not sufficient to see the teacher-student interaction in class merely as a means to transfer professional knowledge. Rather, teaching and learning in the studio can be seen as a dyadic pedagogical relationship, wherein the teacher supports the student's overall development with pedagogic knowledge. From the viewpoint of attachment theory, teachers act in class as secondary attachment figures. They can provide secure attachment to their students in order to foster their self-efficacy, autonomy in learning and exploration.
This approach broadens the set of necessary teaching skills to include, besides professional expertise, also soft skills such as: criticality, self-regulation and versatility. These social skills are not a given; they have to be gained and honed. This presentation would like to discuss the enhancement of the teachers' introspective competence by professionally developing their reflexivity. Findings stemming from attachment theory may provide a framework, from which the teacher's pre-reflective self-awareness may be transformed into professional knowledge. This may also be a valid starting point to motivate teachers to engage in practitioner's research in the field of studio teaching. By conducting research on their own professional practice, studio teachers may gain new insights in their educational role, become aware of their responsibilities as attachment figures and find additional skills for their future practice.

**Katharina Schilling-Sandvoß / Anselma Lanzendörfer (Hochschule für Musik und Darstellende Kunst Frankfurt am Main)**

## Discovering Music: A Cooperative Project between Music University, Schools and Concert Hall

In the course of one semester, music teaching students of the University of Music and Performing Arts Frankfurt develop workshops focusing on selected concerts of the "Alte Oper Frankfurt". These workshops are then held in secondary school classes. Their aim is to practice active music listening and to explore music through creative involvement. The highlight of the project is a shared concert visit at the "Alte Oper", where pupils get to experience the music live.
By involving different institutions, the project aims for several goals: Pupils have the opportunity to visit high-quality concerts and to take part in a cultural event. Their previous active engagement with the music enables a more attentive concert experience. At the same time, the workshops add to the regular music lessons and support a central aim of music education in schools: to enable pupils to have a self-determined contact with music of different eras, cultures, and styles. Future music teachers are offered the opportunity to plan their own music lessons und to test methods of active music listening in a teaching situation. "Alte Oper" can extend its education program by offering a series of workshops to secondary schools.
The project was evaluated through a questionnaire addressed to the pupils. Its main focus was an assessment of the workshops, but it also asked about the level of recognition of the music during the concerts. The evaluation showed that the methods applied in the workshops intensified the listening experiences of the pupils during the live performance.
In our presentation of this project, which will take place for the second time in the winter of 2016/2017, we discuss the general conditions, the different teaching methods in the workshops, and the results of the evaluation, as well as our experiences with challenges and opportunities in this kind of institutional collaboration.

**Lili Schutte (Conservatory of Amsterdam)**

## It Takes Two to Teach Music

We all agree that high-quality music education is needed in primary education. But who should teach music to secure certain standards? Should this be the specialist music teacher or the generalist teacher, or could it not be both? Each, from his/her perspective, might be able to add to the quality of music education because both have specific skills that can be combined.
This poses the question: Why should we not start a joint course for pre-service generalist teachers and pre-service music teachers and encourage them to work together? Our project "It takes 2 to teach music" explored and researched the co-teaching approach with students of the Conservatory of Amsterdam and students of three Amsterdam Pabos (generalist teacher training) within the period 2014 to 2016. The co-teaching model made students design, execute and reflect upon a music lesson *together*: Each person participated in the design and teaching process, using his/her knowledge, skills and teaching experience.

In this presentation we will show why this unique collaboration between the Conservatory of Amsterdam and the three Pabos in Amsterdam was initiated and how the gap between different perspectives on how to teach music was closed using co-teaching and peer-learning. We will share the outcomes of this project and indicate the follow-up.

**Pinar Besevli Solmaz (Ondokuz Mayıs University, Samsun) /**
**Gülin Öziskender (Ondokuz Mayıs University, Samsun)**

## An Assessment of the "Black Sea Meets Vienna" Project

This study presents the "Black Sea Meets Vienna" project which was prepared and applied using experienced learning models – emphasizing doing, living, watching, observing, feeling and thinking. The project is carried out by amateur volunteer students, who have been taking private piano lessons in Samsun located in the Black Sea region of Turkey, their parents and teachers. The participant students were between the ages of six and sixteen, their performance levels ranged from beginners to advanced learners. The project took place in Vienna from June 18th to June 23rd 2016 for the purpose of expanding music culture acquisition, musical style, knowledge and musical experience for participants based on the theory of constructivism. The students had the chance to get immersed in the Viennese culture, they received amateur music education and to find out the level of their coeval colleagues in Vienna were invited to perform in a joint concert. Another objective was to inform students and their parents about the history of music and art by providing them with the opportunity to observe different forms of artistic expression like paintings, architecture, sculpture, landscape architecture, and also to experience their relation to and interaction with music. With this approach not only the students who were receiving amateur music education, but also their parents and teachers gained information and got involved in cultural experiences. This project aims at bringing together different cultures with the help of the universal language of music. In this study, processes, methods, ways of realizing our ideas and the results of the "Black Sea Meets Vienna" project will be presented.

**Suyun Tang (MOE, Singapore)**

## An Inter-Art Approach to Develop a Seeing Ear and Hearing Eye

A mono-artistic pedagogical approach limits accessibility to music education. Not all students will be receptive or can make an immediate connection with music learning. The inter-art project was introduced this year to the lower secondary General Music Program students to reduce the limitation of a mono-artistic pedagogical approach.
This inter-art project was spurred by two beliefs: (1) that drawing and doodling is a natural skill for these youngsters; (2) an inter-art approach would provide greater accessibility to the teaching and learning of musical concepts than a mono-artistic curriculum.
One of the primary aims of this pedagogical approach is to allow the less musically inclined students to realize how visual art and music are connected and are an integral part in our daily lives. This pedagogical approach is also aimed at developing the students' innate sense of 'seeing sounds' and 'hearing the picture'.
Students make use of technology, art and music to learn musical concepts. Both visual art and music are used as stimulus or point of departure. In the first phase, students doodle or draw their response to a musical extract or musical element. In the second phase, students create a programmatic piece of music stimulated by a single frame picture.
This approach will allow students to be more confident in discussing their musical responses. The sharing of visual artworks with the audience provides greater understanding of how different musical responses can be. Students also become more sensitized to the sounds around them shaping their daily lives. Creativity is also called to the fore in the invitation to compose a sonic story as stimulated by an artwork. Students will learn how sonic sensibility can tell an imaginative story.

Maura Thornton (Hibernia College, Dublin) / Kate Heneghan (Dublin)

## "Westport-Scoil-Cheoil": An (Ad)Venture that Explores Multiple Facets of Transmission in Irish-Traditional-Music

The role, function and place of Irish traditional music are now significant issues in the Irish primary school because the contemporary Irish education curriculum espouses a liberal, multicultural/intercultural approach to music education at the expense of Irish traditional music. This paper draws on findings from Maura Thornton's recent qualitative research which concludes that Irish traditional music in Irish primary school education is in crisis: the majority of teachers feel they are not adequately trained to deliver it, are under-confident and do not have time in an over-crowded curriculum. The result is: Many pupils in Irish primary schools may not even be exposed to Irish music thus neglecting a significant aspect of Irish culture. As a response to these challenging findings and in order to address some of the exigent issues Thornton and Heneghan established a new (ad)venture in Irish traditional music "Westport-Scoil-Cheoil" (Westport-Music-School) in 2014. Attendance at this week long summer school in July is officially recognized as CPD (Continuous Professional Development) for teachers by the Irish Government, The Department of Education and Skills. Attendance, is not however, confined to teachers. Many people from diverse nationalities attend, with ages ranging from 4 to 84! The aim of the week long music school in the beautiful, historic Atlantic coastal town of Westport is not only to pass on Irish traditional music but to transmit the music using the aural and visual aspects of transmission without using written notation. Thus, innovative, challenging, yet ancient pedagogical approaches to teaching Irish traditional music are in evidence in Westport. The school is in its third year: so far 'pupils' (a significant number of participants, of course, are primary school teachers) report learning music using this methodology liberating. The school hires the most renowned Irish traditional musicians in the world to pass on their expertise in Irish music in a week long immersion programme. The school caters for absolute beginners to the very skilled traditional musician.

Zsuzsanna Hegedűsné Tóth (Eötvös Loránd University, Budapest)

## "Music in Everything": A Novel Approach in Teaching Music to Young Children Using their Creativity

The aim of the paper is to present a music educational method which was developed by the author in 2012 with the purpose of helping the musical education of children aged two to six and seven to nine. The programme, based on the method named "Tesz-Vesz Muzsika" ("Active Music"), has been running in MÜPA (a leading cultural institution in Budapest) and other venues. A collection of activities used in the sessions was published in a book in 2016 *(Music in Everything: A Collection of Ideas for Games Used in the "Tesz-Vesz" Music Programme to Support the Musical Self-Fulfilment of Children Aged 3 to 9).*

The method is based on the music pedagogical concepts of Zoltán Kodály, Katalin Forrai, Klára Kokas and László Sáry. It assumes that all children have the ability to understand music and express themselves through it. In the music sessions toys, everyday objects (clothespins, buttons, chopsticks, swatters, etc.) and objects of other areas (sport cones, coordination ladders, building blocks, etc.) are used in the musical development activities in unusual, and sometimes surprising ways. The method focuses on children's own experience and playful perception. Children can spontaneously discover the building blocks of music: tempo, rhythm, dynamics, tonality, melody, harmony, texture, tone colour as well as the joy of playing music and doing activities together. It can result in the appearance of such activities in children's free playing time outside the sessions as well. The difficulty of the activities can be changed gradually, thus offering opportunities for differentiation and adaptive development, and the method can also function as a bridge between kindergarten and school.

The use of everyday objects in the musical activities enhances children's motivation, their creative thinking and problem-solving skills, and therefore contributes to the development of various abilities in addition to musical competences.

**Sabina Vidulin (Music Academy in Pula, University of Juraj Dobrila in Pula)**

## The Collaboration between School, Music Associations and Town Institutions: What Does a Student Acquire?

The identification of different models for school modernization is an important segment of practitioners' and scientists' work commitment. Opening the school to the partnership is a model for educational improvement. Newman (2002) and Previšić (2012) point out that the expansion of school activities with the opportunities provided by the extracurricular environment results in the complete transformation of students' knowledge and skills. Since the introduction of cultural and artistic achievements is one of the most important tasks of education (Hermann, 2004; Vidulin-Orbanić, 2013) special attention should be attached to the enrichment of students' school and out-of-school time.
The intention of the author is to present the possibilities of cultural network and collaborations between schools and private music and non-music associations. The educational project "Music Theorem" and three children's choral festivals are analyzed, with the intention to determine what competencies the students acquire in one extended educational process. "Music Theorem" is a cycle of educational concerts for students of compulsory school, conducted by a private association which provides an opportunity to live music experiences and talks with the artists and composers. Analyzing the concerts' programs, we have noticed that they partly coincide with the music syllabus for compulsory school and offer a possibility to learn music outside of school and to experience different types of music.
In order to popularize choral singing and pick out talented students, the projects of school, town and county singing festivals for students, in cooperation with schools and partners (private music associations and the town) have been revealed successful. Students had the opportunity to develop their singing skill, make music in collaboration with other artists, which also had a great impact on their social and emotional development.
These examples are the proof that school, with the partners' support, has influenced the advancement of the students' cultural and artistic identity. The collaboration between school, associations and other institutions contributes to a better understanding of music and affects active students' participation in the musical life of the community.

**Michaela Weinhauser (University of Music and Performing Arts Munich) / Franziska Böhm (Munich)**

## A Body-Oriented Constructivist Approach to Music Learning: Exploring Different Metres and Rhythm Polyphony through Movement, Voice and Instruments

The study reports on an artistic-pedagogical team-teaching project with thirteen to fourteen year old pupils of a secondary school in Munich, Germany, and focuses on the practical application of constructivist learning theories within the context of music and movement education in schools.
We are two students of Elemental Music Education at the University of Music and Performing Arts in Munich and once a week over three months we worked with the eighth graders. The learning contents were based on the Bavarian curriculum for Gymnasium. Key activities were dance and music improvisation, choreography, body percussion and percussion, composition with different meters and rhythm polyphony.
Constructivist theories about learning suggest that individuals react differently to objective influences, as different senses, physiological, neural, cognitive and social processes are activated. Thereby subjective learning experiences are created, whereby the learning contents can be stored differently. These views are also applicable to music learning, based on a body-oriented approach to rhythm, in particular to the phenomenon of metre change.
In this presentation we aim to show the learning contents, analyse the teaching as well as the pedagogic strategies and reflect on the constructivist approach in practice. Here the emphasis is on the connection between knowledge about music theory and the bodily-kinaesthetic experience of the students in the process of musical exploration, improvisation and composition.
The focus will be on the social, musical and physical learning conditions which were needed to develop and channel the individual learning process as well as the students' independent learning.
The methodological/didactic approach was based on Wilfried Gruhn's (1998) sequential learning model (listening, exploring, experimenting, articulating, naming, writing), which we believe led to an effective bodily-based representation of the rhythmic structures. Building on this pedagogical foundation, the learners involved in the project experienced interdisciplinary approaches as well as some intercultural examples about the theme of different metres and rhythm polyphony.

**Zhang Wenzhuo (Fredonia, New York)**

## Integrated Multicultural Music Education: Pedagogies and Practices Using Chinese Music as a Model

Integrated multicultural music education associates learning music with various other disciplines. By using Chinese music as a model, the aim of this paper is to provide insights into pedagogies that draw upon the theory of transfer of learning and engage both attentive and engaged listening skills to enrich learning experiences in multicultural music study.

This paper emphasizes 'specific transfer' and 'general transfer' in regard to the theory of transfer of learning. 'Specific transfer' takes place between study areas sharing many similarities. Music study can be incorporated with history classes, social sciences, literature, cultural studies, and even certain TV programs. 'General transfer' focuses on the learners' cognitive and social abilities. Music classes based on the general transfer theory would address students' developing mindfulness, perception, and problem-solving abilities in order that they employ their capabilities to complete tasks in other domains within or outside school. Ideally, school-based music classes interact with community-based arts organizations, such as orchestras, museums, and music groups, in order to enrich students' learning experience by utilizing their previous knowledge in various new settings. My presentation will use Chinese music as an example to discuss the specific methods and potential challenges to apply those theories in practice in an academic setting.

Listening is a key activity to develop students' sound awareness and their conceptual understanding of music regarding its use and meaning in other people's lives and cultural traditions. The paper introduces 'attentive listening', which emphasizes rhythmic patterns, contours of melodies, keys, scales, music forms, instrumentation, and cultural contexts beyond the music; and 'engaged listening', which inspires students' creativity in music-making. Specific musical activities and instructional methods employing these two listening methods will be discussed by using Chinese music as an example.

**Motje Wolf / Sarah Younie (De Montfort University Leicester)**

## Enabling Access: Translating Music Education Research for Practitioners

Not only is conducting and publishing research slow, but the process of implementing research findings into schools is even slower. Often, vital findings are hidden behind pay walls or in long academic articles. Therefore, they are difficult to access by teachers and other educational professionals. The "MESHGUIDES" project (Mapping Educational Specialist KnowHow) answers this problem by providing concise research summaries to allow teachers to access the latest findings and thereby improve their own practice.

MESHGuides are an example of translational research. Translational research is a well-established concept in medicine; however, it is less well developed in the education sector. Translational research is a systematic approach that turns research knowledge into practical applications. The MESH project translates the findings of educational research into practical outcomes for classroom teachers in the form of short summaries or flow charts.

In this talk, we would like to introduce the music strand for the MESHGuides. We will be introducing a first design of the Music MESHGuides platform and prototypes of currently developed Music MESHguides.

The method of providing MESHGuides presents an innovative and groundbreaking way of publishing that reaches a wider audience than just academic colleagues. Therefore, it also opens the opportunity for co-research in schools as teachers are invited to share their best practice through MESHGuides.

A small number of music MESHGuides is currently in preparation, ready to be shared at the conference and open for discussion, feedback and further development.

We would like to take the opportunity at this conference to create an international MESHGuides music education community with the aim to set up an editorial board with international editors and reviewers. This is an invitation to get involved.

Katervna Zavalko (National Pedagogical Dragomanov University, Kyiv)

## "Music-Children" Project: Mastering Playing in a Chamber Orchestra by Primary School Children

The "music-children" project, which took place during the academic years 2013 to 2016 (experimental laboratory at National Pedagogical Dragomanov University, Kyiv, Ukraine), brought together fifteen violinists and cellists aged six to ten. It was developed with the help of an experimental curriculum, based on the musical and pedagogical concepts of Carl Orff, Zoltán Kodály, Émile Jaques-Dalcroze and violin teaching methods by Géza Szilvay and S. Miltonyan, which aimed at attracting children to play in a chamber orchestra and promote the skills of playing violin and cello. According to the curriculum, each child should attend orchestral lessons once a week and participate in creative projects (violin summer camps, concerts, festivals).

The learning process took place in two stages: Stage 1 (lasted for the first year) – mastering the basics of orchestral music, skills of playing in a music ensemble and reading orchestral scores; Stage 2 (second and third years) – playing at the orchestral lessons.

With the aim to facilitate and motivate novice students the special program of joint music making in orchestral lessons was developed, since the initial period of learning to play the bowed string instruments is one of the most difficult. Orchestral lessons have their own specifics, due to physiological characteristics of novice students as well as a limited set of technical skills.

During orchestral lessons attention was being paid to the development of musical and performing skills, sense of rhythm, ear for music, musical thinking, and motor coordination. Utilization of music games for the development of coordination, sense of rhythm and ear for music brought diversity to the lesson.

The positive results of the project are: students' motivation to improve their own violin and cello playing skills have been formed; skills of reading sheet music have been mastered; their sense of rhythm and musical ear has been improved; experience in public performance has been gained; skills of nonverbal communication and teamwork have been mastered; autonomy and responsibility have been promoted.

Anette Ziegenmeyer (University of Wuppertal)

## "KulturCampus Wuppertal" (KCW): An Interdisciplinary Project by Annette Ziegenmeyer and Björn Krüger

"KCW" is based on an interdisciplinary approach supporting students of the University of Wuppertal (starting with the Faculty of Music Education) to actively shape and model the cultural scene in the city of Wuppertal.

Based on the assumption that today, creative and innovative concepts are more important than capital, "KCW" helps students to develop, elaborate and realize their own cultural projects by providing them with the necessary skills and by networking with cultural institutions and local artists.

"KCW" hast just recently started (September 2016) and the first cycle will last about three years (September 2016 to September 2019). It is financed by the University of Wuppertal, the FABU and the "Jackstädtstiftung".

Weekly meetings led by Annette Ziegenmeyer and Björn Krüger are based on the followings steps: First, the students will explore the current cultural situation in Wuppertal. Based on their findings (What are the possible needs for the various cultural activities?), the students will develop and elaborate their own ideas for future cultural projects. In this phase, they will receive insight on relevant topics such as how to write a project application and how to elaborate a project design including a solid expense budget. Furthermore, they will learn about possibilities of local networking. "KCW" in this context will create a non-profit association to ensure the successful realization of the different projects. The following aims and perspectives determine our activities:

(1) "KCW" wants to encourage students to create and develop new cultural impulses in the city.
(2) By trying out their project ideas in real funding programs (e.g. "Bergischer Kulturfonds"), the students can experience all the crucial points and possible pitfalls of working in the cultural domain. Furthermore, they get a chance to build networks and discover career opportunities and also find fields of research (according to the diverse projects).
(3) Finally, "KCW" is going to document and evaluate the process of project development (how to create ideas and turn theoretical knowledge into practice) so that it can grow and become a solid institution at the University of Wuppertal and serve as a model.

**Jereon Vanesser (UCLL, Leuven Limburg)**

## Music Teacher or Music Educator

Art and culture have been redefined in the last decades. A social component is now an indispensable and essential condition when talking about art and culture. Also hybridism, interdisciplinarity and global dialogue have become main features. Fortunately, education in the fields of art and culture is influenced by these developments.

Music education in schools should, therefore, evolve towards more multidimensionality, interdisciplinarity and become more oriented towards establishing connections, preferably organized in different contexts, both within and outside the school walls.

The process of change which our students have to undergo, if they want to remain up to date and 'socially relevant', requires an evolution within the subject pedagogy (methodology): Until now, we have been educating mono-disciplinary art teachers for schools, whereas our society is asking for multidisciplinary artistic music educators. The difference between the two types of teachers is the social engagement and the ability (competences) to work in a multidisciplinary way. So, it is quite problematic that those competences are not reflected in the current curriculum although the current teacher profile requires them.

This is why we experimented in the art-department of our lower secondary teacher education at UCLL and developed a community-art project. "The Singing Table" enables our students to explore and apply the possibilities of vocal music making, which they have acquired in our teacher education, in order to enhance the relevance of their social role. When singing together they experience the powerful musical and social experience promoted by a group. In other words, they are taught how they can apply music and singing together in a social context to solve problems. In my lecture I wish to report on this process, both with words and images.

# WORKSHOPS

Markus Detterbeck (Helbling Verlagsgesellschaft m.b.H.)

## Pop Choral Singing in School- and Youth-Choirs

How can I achieve a snappy groove with my school or youth choir, why is the beat so important, and how can I find the right sound for a particular song? To answer these questions, we will work on elements specific to pop choral singing, such as the phrasing typical of the style, groove, vocussion, articulation, vocal timbre and vocal balance.
In the workshop, we will first look at possible ways of building up the vocal abilities of the singers in the choir and achieving lasting improvement by means of targeted warming up exercises. Practice materials include chants, 'stimmicals' (a form of warming-up exercise that consists of short musical motifs), canons, or also body percussion pieces, that not only build up the singers' abilities but are also fun.
In a further step, we shall work on a number of examples of groovy choral arrangements from the rock-pop sphere and also from Africa, whose levels of difficulty and required formations make them suitable for work with school- and youth-choirs.
In addition there will be tips for the direction of pop choirs: presence and contact with the group, groove-oriented conducting, efficient entrances/downbeats/fermata, and conducting that supports vocal techniques.

Rosa de las Heras Fernández (UNIR Universidad Internacional de la Rioja, Madrid)

## Introduction to Flamenco in a Primary Classroom

Flamenco style has remained outside educational contexts such as primary education, even though this music is ascribed to the objectives, content and competencies of the Spanish official curriculum of Primary Education. Besides, the way of learning flamenco music has traditionally been orally, through observation, imitation and repetition. This way of teaching and learning fails to address the knowledge and understanding that all this learning requires. This study aims to show a didactic proposal for the introduction to flamenco in the school curriculum of primary education. It is designed according to the official Spanish curriculum. It also aims to show some teaching resources for learning the rhythms of flamenco music. Some of these resources have been adapted from those proposed by different musical pedagogues. Different rhythm and movement activities in various flamenco styles as well as exercises for auditory recognition and motor skills, with marches, palms and feet movements are displayed. The workshop will be held in open space with music and participants do not need prior knowledge. For these activities you should wear comfortable clothing. The conclusions show that proposed adaptations of musical teaching methods can be resources for knowledge and understanding of the rhythm of flamenco music and their possible introduction into the elementary classroom.

Fritz Höfer (University of Education Salzburg)

## Computer and Tablet Support in 'Classroom Music'

Many new curricula for teaching music in secondary school require a re-orientation of the subject, meaning that in a lot of cases the focus has shifted to music making in the classroom (in the course of the abstract referred to as 'classroom music') involving all pupils. Moreover, the significance of digital media in music education has been discussed frequently in recent years. The connection of these two topics leads to the question if teaching classroom music can be supported through the use of computers and tablets.
There are many possibilities: computer apps that can substitute musical instruments, web 2.0 applications that support working together on compositions, or the use of computer programs for sequencing and arranging music, which can be a helpful tool in rehearsing classroom music arrangements.
In addition, there is a lot of potential in the combination of different media (e.g. different forms of visualizing music) and in controlling and accessing music through computers and tablets.
Just as it is necessary for music teachers to master certain instruments, especially the piano or the guitar, to be able to teach music adequately, the use of software and various apps supporting the learning process in music should also be seen as a necessary requirement for teachers, especially in the area of classroom music.

A lot of new aids concerning singing and classroom music are becoming accessible for teachers, who manage to use computers and tablets effectively during their lessons. I will present software and apps which support and help practicing classroom music: for example, a dynamic playback of a sequencing software, which allows the user to select tracks and control the tempo, can help the teacher when working on percussion patterns with his students.
The format of the presentation will be a mixture of demonstration and workshop. Participants will be invited to use some of the applications discussed while making music with instruments that are easy to handle (boomwhackers, mallets, percussion ...).
An insight in the following areas will be given:

- interactive flash scores,
- Noteflight Online Notation,
- sequencing software: Studio One Prime,
- Apple Garage Band,
- Drum Machine App,
- Chord App (Arranger App)
- Band in a Box Arranger Software.

**Panagiota Papageorgiou (National and Kapodistrian University of Athens)**

## Connecting Music with the Study of People and Cultures through Active Experiences with World Music: The Example of a Maori Stick Game-Song

World music can combine music learning with learning about different places, eras, people, and cultures, while helping students become aware of the cultural diversity that characterizes the world, as well as music itself. Learning about the role of music in other cultures' customs and ceremonies also encourages respect of diversity, thus helping students become better citizens in contemporary multicultural societies. At the same time, world music provides ample opportunities for multisensory learning and can be combined with innovative and enjoyable activities that engage students actively in the musical processes and refine their aural and motor skills.
This workshop aims to show how such a combination of integrative, active and enjoyable learning can be achieved in the classroom, using the example of the Maori stick game-song "E Papa Waiari". In traditional Maori society, males and females of all ages used to play stick games (called 'ti rakau' or 'titi torea'), in which players, usually sitting in pairs or rows, rhythmically threw and caught sticks in time to a chant or song. Apart from providing entertainment, these games were also intended to train young Maori warriors in spear fighting, help them practice hand-eye coordination, and teach them rhythm and synchronization.
In the workshop, participants will learn the song "E Papa Waiari" and perform it in combination with rhythmic patterns played with a pair of wooden sticks, according to the Maori tradition. They will also be introduced to some facts about the Maori history and culture, explore the role of music and games as entertainment in the Maori culture, and watch related videos.
Music educators participating in this workshop will be provided with ideas about how world music can integrate musical and cultural knowledge, promote active and multisensory learning, and also make the lesson a fun experience.

**Sven Stagge (Yamaha Music Europe GmbH.)**

## Keyboard*Class*

The keyboard is one of the most used instruments in schools. It has been developed into a 'complete' musical instrument, allowing students to play music with a wide variety of sounds in different styles. Keyboards can play a key role in providing children with comprehensive basic musicality as well as ensemble playing skills or in accompanying singers or other instrumentalists.
Accordingly, KeyboardClass as a teaching method serves several purposes.
On the one hand, it leads to production-oriented music education. By touching the keys of the keyboard, students can - literally speaking - 'grasp' important aspects of music theory. On top of that, the keyboard also lets you teach instrumentation in a more motivating way, and it opens up great opportunities for musical creativity – everyone plays the same instrument.

On the other hand, the method systematically encourages playing special class ensemble arrangements. It is designed for grades 5 and 6 in middle schools or for grades 3 and 4 in primary schools.
In the workshops, you will get to know the teaching materials KeyboardClass as well as the specialised teaching methods for music ensembles in the classroom. The participants will play on state-of-the-art keyboards. No special previous knowledge is required.

**Johannes Treß (Pädagogische Hochschule, Freiburg)**

## "(How) Can I Learn to Improvise?" A Multidimensional Approach to Improvisation in Practice

"Teaching is inherently improvisational" (Burnard, 2013). Improvisational processes need an immense focus on developing and reflecting interactive rules of engagement. Being the one, who improvises is one thing. But being the instructor of a group improvisation is something even more challenging (Gagel, 2010). The workshop will give you the possibility to play both roles. Together we will shed light on the challenges and possibilities of group improvisation and the special role of 'leading' improvisational sessions. We will get to know different improvisation approaches and explore teaching ideas and materials. The main focus of the workshop will be reflecting on the individual practical experiences. The workshop refers to the presentation of my research paper. Own instruments are welcome but not necessary.

**Francis Dubé (Laval University, Québec) / Astrid Marin (Laval University, Québec) / Jean-Philippe Després (Laval University, Québec)**

## Designing Non-Digital Music Mini-Games WITH and FOR Students

Games are an effective learning approach (Jun-Mei, 2011) that places learners into an inquiry-based complex problem-solving space in which challenges are 'scaffolded' to capture their attention for a certain period of time (Idriss Aberrante, 2016; Stott & Neustaedter, 2013). Consequently, student learning outcomes are significantly greater when they are learning with a game-based approach as opposed to standard instruction (Clark, Tanner-Smith & Killingsworth, 2013). One key challenge of 21st century education is to design learning environments that take full advantage of the core mechanics of game play (Paras, 2005) to increase student engagement and achievement simultaneously. In order to do so, the educational games should preferably originate in the minds of the students themselves, and should then be developed in collaboration with other students and their teachers (Prensky, 2008). In fact, the educational games created by educators 'smell' too much like school (Lim, 2008), and lessen the students' propensity to identify with the game. In other words, if students aren't having any input into the creation of their own educational games, odds are high that they will find them relatively boring.
This workshop aims to help music teachers working in diverse educational contexts to build original non-digital music mini-games in a collaborative process with their students, by including them as co-designers, play testers and rollout supporters. As explained by Prensky (2008), mini-games take less than an hour to play, are generally centered on a single, narrow subject, and may have multiple levels. They also are the most sustainable type of games for practitioners because they can be easily implemented within the time frame of a lesson. During the workshop, the participants will be invited to design and test one non-digital music mini-game, and will be provided empowering informative tools to create novel games *with* and *for* their students.

**Anna Gritsch (Vienna)**

## Body Music

Body music resources are extremely versatile tools for music teaching. They are applicable with any target group, under any given circumstances, without any specific materials and for any desired purpose. Apart from the musical richness, they offer playful possibilities for training crucial skills like perception, coordination, independence, simultaneity of listening and doing, pulsation, spontaneous reaction and creativity.
This workshop offers a glimpse into this universe of sounds, rhythms and interactions. The focus lies less on studying ready-made grooves and arrangements but in discovering the potential that lies in the skill of combining a certain

number of parameters to fit the moment. Balancing repetition and variation, exploring different sets of rules for improvisations, co-creating music with the full spectrum of bodily resources, welcoming chaos and 'misunderstandings', developing non-verbal instructions and creating a positive learning environment, are some of the chapters of the book that we are going to write in this workshop. Of course, there will also be room for discussion and reflection.

**Gerhard Lock (Tallinn University, Baltic Film, Media, Arts and Communication School) / Marit Mõistlik-Tamm (Tallinn University)**

## 'All Together Now!': Five Inspiring Steps towards Adventurous Musical Co-Creation

Our belief is that everybody is musical and can engage in improvisation at some level (MacDonald & Wilson, 2014) as well as in composing in general. It is crucial to develop this confidence in music students and pupils. These principles have been developed and practically applied in the school project "Querklang" in Berlin for about ten years. In autumn 2016 "Querklang Goes Europe" (QUEU) Comenius project started networking in six European countries (Germany, Austria, Belgium, Greece, Portugal, Estonia) joining together higher music education institutions and schools to share musical experiences internationally.

During a 90-min workshop we will introduce a step-by-step plan for supervising the process of musical co-creation:

(1) exploring the environment and everyday sounds;
(2) experiencing colours, shapes and words;
(3) creating a graphic score;
(4) translating the score into music;
(5) recording and reflecting the final performance.

Based on our course "Practice of Musical Co-Creation", we focus on supporting and developing the student's readiness for musical co-creation aiming at

(1) creating opportunities for developing students as creative team leaders (initiators) & members (co-authors), and
(2) supporting the formation of musical co-creation through various impulses as symbols/triggers.

The workshop will concentrate on central aspects important for building a successful course including assessment issues. Our plan can be extended or foreshortened over a period of time as needed by the teacher. We believe that our concept provides a safe environment to take challenges and benefits of interdisciplinary and multimedia approaches. Within the QUEU project our experiences will contribute to a deeper understanding of musical co-creation and how to support future music educators.

**Peter Mall / Ralf-Olivier Schwarz (Hochschule für Musik und Darstellende Kunst, Frankfurt am Main)**

## School, Outreach and Community: Perspectives on Cross-Institutional Music Education

Music education takes place in and outside the classroom. Symphony orchestras, concert halls, opera companies etc. cooperate with schools; community music projects offer educational opportunities far beyond official curricula. Networking has become an everyday challenge for music educators. Yet in everyday business, dialogue between the different actors often is difficult and hardly effective (Mall, 2016).

Sociological approaches provide effective tools for describing, analyzing and understanding communities of (musical) practice. In this sense, formal music education in schools and informal music education in outreach activities or community projects act within different "systems" (Luhmann, 1995 & 2002), respectively in different "fields" (Bourdieu, 1992 & 1996).

In this workshop, we will take a deeper look into the musical communities in different cities, starting with our own experiences of bringing together different musical and/or educational institutions in Frankfurt. The outside view on the very different situation in San Francisco will provide us a contrasting perspective.

The workshop seeks to sensitize the participants for the different backgrounds of practitioners in the arts system and/or the education system. Together we use sociological approaches to analyze different (language) codes, in order to develop a common understanding of different communities of (musical) practice.

**Johannes Steiner (Institute for Music Education, Innsbruck)**

## A Cappella Grooving: A New Way of Singing Pop Songs in Class

The workshop presents possibilities of initiating musical processes with groups and tries to emphasize rhythm singing. "A Cappella Grooving" is a new singing concept for choirs and pupils in class with a focus on popular music and jazz. "A Cappella Grooving" combines body grooves with singing and transfers the principles of making music in bands to a singing group. The combination leads to a holistic approach to music and trains the rhythmical accuracy of the singers. The singers learn how to sing precisely in time.
The body-grooves are developed from the natural movements of the human body. Body grooves are a special form of body percussion technique that emphasizes the movement of the body. They are very helpful in school: They can be used immediately, they are not too loud and the rhythmic patterns can be transferred to voice, other objects or even instruments.
In the beginning, we will start with body groove. Then the participants will learn the bass line. Afterwards, the movements of the body grooves and the patterns will be put together before the participants finally learn the whole song. The main method for learning the piece is called "arranging in pulse", which means that the meter will not stop for the whole studying process. Finally, the choir will work on the the background vocals.

**Sonja Stibi (Mozarteum University Salzburg)**

## From Canon to Creation

Creative learning, group learning and cooperative music-making in heterogeneous groups are at the core of the Orff approach. Following the traces of music and dance we will change from singing to vocussion (vocal percussion), from body percussion to movement, from fixed repertoire to improvisation and creation. Body sounds and sounding gestures will lead to rhythmic accompaniment as well as to dance forms. Within the interplay of instructed and explorative-creative parts and using the methods of Elemental Music and Dance Pedagogy, the workshop shows ways of connecting music, movement and voice in a playful and creative way.
Please bring comfortable clothes. Your instruments are welcome.

**Psyrra Vasiliki (University of Music Franz Liszt, Weimar)**

## Music Begins Where Words End

Apart from being a basic part of cultural education, music also provides a wide range of methodological approaches that can support skills and knowledge acquisition in general. The aims of the workshop are:
(1) to provide educational material and methodologies for school and out-of-school learning, which focus on language acquisition and inclusion and
(2) to strengthen and support the existing pedagogical approaches in general, while aiming at changing children's critical thinking, promoting cultural participation of every child and encouraging inclusion.
The workshop is encouraging the participants to enrich their pedagogical material and learn how to transfer this knowledge according to their strengths and needs. The content of the workshop will include:
(1) non-verbal communication with the children,
(2) inclusion of the language of the region of origin,
(3) musical-cultural specifics and characteristics of origin (rhythmical patterns, scales, musical forms genres, dances etc.).
Through this workshop we will have the chance to open a dialogue about the cultural interchange and network, as well as the diversity in our present society. Children's musical practices and needs are heterogeneous in many ways – even if their biological age is the same: biological equipment, interests, regional, social and cultural origins differ. Diversity is part of living together. Music practice offers many opportunities to express heterogeneity and diversity artistically, and to give every child the opportunity to express himself/herself.

# SYMPOSIA AND FORUMS

## Doctoral Student Forum – Poster Presentation

**Chairs: Mary Stakelum (GBR), Thade Buchborn (GER)**

The Doctoral Student Forum provides doctoral students, at any stage of their studies, an opportunity to present, share, and discuss their work in a supportive environment. The forum sessions include peer led discussion and workshops given by Dr. Mary Stakelum (Bath Spa University, UK) and Prof. Dr. Thade Buchborn (University of Music Freiburg, Germany) and culminate in a dedicated DSF poster session at the conference where each participant is invited to make a public presentation of their poster and to get some valuable feedback from conference delegates.

## Joint Musical (Ad)ventures in Europe: Looking for Partners for Comparative Research and Practice Projects

**National Coordinators' Symposium**

This symposium invites participants to come together in joint musical adventures, aiming to establish close collaboration and network systems among EAS National coordinators and other interested EAS members. Current research studies or practice projects conducted by members of the National Coordinators group in their countries will be presented, inviting interested colleagues to join in, in an attempt to look at them from a comparative perspective lens and adapt them to other national educational contexts.
Up to six projects will be presented and each presentation will last around five to six minutes, followed by a 45-minute discussion within break-out groups (based on the topics presented). Each group will consist of the NCs and other interested collaborators. The symposium will end with a 15- minute general discussion for all persons attending the symposium.
Hopefully this symposium will instigate some meaningful and fruitful collaboration among NCs and other interested EAS members and that it will mark the beginning in the establishment of working groups within our NCs' group based on our common interest in music education research and practice.

**Christopher Wallbaum (Music University, Leipzig) Christian Rolle (University of Köln), Sarah Hennessy (University of Exeter), Olle Zandén (Linnaeus University), Daniel Prantl (Hochschule für Musik und Theater "Felix Mendelssohn Bartholdy" Leipzig), Simon Stich (University of Köln)**

## Comparing Music Lessons: The Application of Different Guiding Ideas

The general idea of the symposium is to present two lessons, structured by the following different guiding ideas:

- enabling experiences (example from Germany),
- learning and evaluating competences (example from Sweden).

The symposium will be opened with a short film from Bavaria, focusing on how a supposedly universal atmosphere emerges in music lessons and a film-sequence from Sweden exemplifying possibilities for learning in music teaching concentrating on goals and results. The participants will eventually be invited to compare the examples with experiences in their own countries. The results of this group work will be shared and the session will be closed with a short film referring to music teaching in China. Thus another perspective will be introduced.

**Georg Steinschaden (Mozarteum University Salzburg) / Ludwig Nussbichler (Musikum Salzburg)**

## Pre-College: A Joint Adventure?

In 2015, the pre-college was established at the Mozarteum University to support gifted young instrumentalists and singers at a very early stage in their development. Apart from instrumental lessons, various courses (including music theory, solfeggio, improvisation and composition, singing etc.) are integrated into the program. The courses are specially designed for the demands of young students who meet at weekends so that their attendance of formal teaching at schools in the closer and wider area of Salzburg is 'undisturbed'. While last year's work involving around 100 students was commended, many questions were also raised.
The presentation, after providing a short insight into basic aims of Pre-College, will focus on a joint adventure: GCC – a guided collective composition. We will try to illustrate the process of composition, involving 25 students of Pre-College, with examples performed by Susila Heath, Irina Schukoff and Halina Ciesielczyk.

## Student Forum

**Chairs: Branka Rotar Pance (SLO), Oliver Krämer (GER)**

The focus of the forum is on giving students the opportunity to share and exchange their experience of and views on music teacher training. In the forum they also explore and discuss issues which have impact on the future of music education in schools and beyond. Students gain insight into each other's ideas, approaches in music education, and the school contexts of the different countries. The key questions are closely connected to the topic of the main conference: Joint (Ad)Venture Music. The hope is that they will discover common ground in their knowledge and understanding, and a better awareness of their own setting. The students have the opportunity to build new friendships all over Europe and to get a place within the EAS network. The forum culminates in a dedicated SF workshop at the conference.

## Interdisziplinarität in der Theorie, Forschung und Praxis der Musikpädagogik der Wyschegrader Länder *(Presentations will partly be in German)*

**Irena Medňanská (University of Prešov) / Miloš Kodejška (Praha) / Marek Sedláček (Brno) / Gabriela Konkol (Gdansk) / Miroslav Dymon (Rzeszow) / Noemi Maczelka (Szeged)**

### The Establishment of New Scientific Disciplines in the Systematics of Music Pedagogy: The Integration of Ideas Derived from Musicology, Pedagogy as Science and Other Social Disciplines and Art

Music pedagogy as a scientific reflection of music-educational processes is differentiated within its internal structure into disciplines linked by content. These are presented in the 'systematics of music pedagogy'. Music pedagogy as a scientific discipline was established in Czechoslovakia in the 1970s thanks to Czech colleagues Frantisek Sedlak (1916–2002), Ivan Polednak (1931–2009) and the Slovakian musicologists Oskar Elschek (1931) and Ladislav Burlas (1927). Ladislav Burlas' systematics, established in Slovakia in the 1990s, represents the following complex of disciplines. They form the core of music pedagogy as a scientific discipline in the system of musicology:
(1) philosophy of music education,
(2) music didactics and methodics,
(3) music-pedagogical psychology,
(4) music-pedagogical sociology,
(5) comparative music pedagogy,
(6) history of music education,
(7) instrumental and vocal pedagogy.
Social changes mirrored in the necessity of theoretical reflection and asking for a new terminology are automatically reflected in music pedagogy as well. Dynamism and openness in music pedagogy create the space for establishing a new discipline expanding into various fields in a cooperation:
(1) with pedagogical science: music andragogy, music geragogy;
(2) with musicology: pedagogical ethnomusicology;
(3) with IT technologies: music-pedagogical informatics;

(4) with religious theory: religious music pedagogy.
New independent subdisciplines are established:
(1) pedagogical musicotherapy (in the educational context)
(2) integrative music pedagogy and polyaesthetic education.
They are the result of the development of music education, globalization, changes within society, family relations and IT progress in the first years of the 21st century. Their existence is dependent on quantitative-qualitative results of music-pedagogical research. Scientific reflection of their significance is necessary for their acceptance in the systematics of music pedagogy.

**Marek Sedláček / Renata Horáková (Masaryk University, Brno)**

### How Do Young People Accept Contemporary Art Music? A Research into Musical Attitudes of University Students in the Czech Republic

Does school music education prepare pupils sufficiently for listening to contemporary classical music? Does an extended music education (elementary art schools) influence musical attitudes, and professional musical practice? The authors of the paper outline the findings of an extensive empirical sociological research carried out nationwide that explored the musical attitudes of university students in the Czech Republic towards classical music of the postmodern period (the last third of the 20th century).
The research was conducted by the Music Department of the Faculty of Education, Masaryk University in Brno, Czech Republic in 2016. It was carried out using a technique which combined an online sound questionnaire and a common questionnaire. 2.081 respondents with compulsory music education, extended music education and professional music education listened to and evaluated twelve pieces of music of the following composers: Arvo Pärt, Pavel Blatný, Helmut Lachenmann, Michal Košut, Ctirad Kohoutek, Henrýk Górecki, Otmar Mácha, Miloslav Ištvan, Steve Reich, Svatopluk Havelka, Olivier Messiaen and Krzysztof Penderecki.
The 'typical respondent' in this research is a woman, aged 22, who received compulsory music education in primary and secondary education. From the selected music examples of the last third of the 20th century, she likes Pärt, Košut, Górecki, Blatný and Ištvan best. The attitudes of respondents who had received an extended and professional music education displayed seemed either more neutral or positive. These test persons were more successful in their attempts at identifying composers (or distinguishing between Czech and foreign music). Based on the results of their research the authors reflect on the possibilities of cooperation between music professionals, art schools and primary schools.

**Noemi Maczelka (University of Szeged) / Irena Medňanská (University of Prešov) / Miroslav Dymon (Rzeszow) / Miloš Kodejška (Praha)**

### Adventures within Music: International Youth Projects in the Music Education Department of Szeged University

It is a valuable and stimulating adventure for young people, belonging to the V4 Group under the tuition of Irena Medňanská, to focus on music by taking part in international projects. This can also include the experience of studying one or more semesters abroad. The Education Faculty of the Szeged University Department of Music focuses on international projects to improve the competences of the students. Besides the bilateral agreements, we offer diverse opportunities including Erasmus Intensive Projects and other international projects, competitions, conferences and mastercourses. In addition to international experiences we focus on the creativity of students and teachers, and attempt at encouraging the students' self determination and proficiency. Future teachers study the Hungarian National Curricula, to explore the different possibilities to improve pupils' creativity. They learn how to combine folk material such as children games with singing, rhythmic movements and folk dance.

**Gabriela Karin Konkol (Faculty of Choral Conducting, Church Music, Artistic Education, Rhythmics and Jazz, Gdansk)**

**Music and Arts Education at *Youth Culture Centers* in Poland**

The "Youth Culture Center" is a municipal institution of extracurricular education. It is one of the most important ones in the Polish national education system. Centers established in this context serve as cultural centers for children and young people in both big and in small cities. They focus, for example, on:

- training and developing children's and young people's interests and talents in art, science and sport;
- providing young people with possibilities of a multidirectional intellectual, spiritual and social development;
- preparing them for conscious and active participation in culture;
- developing the idea of a 'cultural way' of spending leisure time.

Youth Culture Centers also offer special programs for very talented children and for disabled ones. They co-operate with schools, educational, cultural and sports institutions as well as universities. They organize various international and local projects including music festivals, concerts, workshops, performances, competitions and other events. Most of them are members of the National Council of Extracurricular Education.

**Bence Asztalos (University of Szeged)**

**See What You Hear!**

In my poster I will present the Hungarian results of *Musik kreativ+* program: promoting students' creativity and entrepreneurship through classical string quartet music inspired productions. The string quartet helps the development of students' entrepreneurship in the area of arts and arts promoting. The process, in which the students not only listen to the quartet music, but also imagine it and prepare a stage and film production on the basis of the music requires various forms of creativity. The string quartet participates in the realization of the production with the students.

## Platform for Music Teacher Associations (MTA) in Europe

**Main interests, strategies and networks**

During the last years the EAS started to establish a platform for Music Teacher Associations (MTAs) from all over Europe with the aim of creating a network for deeper exchange and supporting the advocacy for music education in schools. At the last EAS-Conference in Vilnius (2016) representatives from European Music Teacher Associations met for the first time in the frame of an EAS conference.

The main reasons for establishing this new platform beside advocacy for music teachers and music education in school will be the work of the Music Teacher Associations themselves, for example the affiliation of members, the organization of unsalaried work and the support of the network of EAS National Coordinators.

In this open session representatives of several European Music Teacher Associations will report and discuss the main issues of an internal meeting, which will take place during this year's EAS-Conference and plan collaborations to strengthen the exchange within this platform . Main topics will be the situation of music education in schools in different countries, best practice of political work and attractive offers for potential members of Music Teacher Associations. The meeting will end in an open discussion on some of these points with the audience.

# POSTERS

Felicity Andreasen (University of Sydney)

## The Use of Objective Measures to Identify and Select Gifted Young Musicians for Specialist Training

During the 1990s, educational reform in Australia altered school management structures and directed curriculum practices towards outcomes – with an emphasis on individual accountability. Within prevailing political and educational landscapes, NSW's first gifted education policy introduced May 1991, revised 2004 outlines a balanced, multivariate approach for identification of gifted and talented students. While Australia is without a National Policy on Gifted and Talented Education (Australian Curriculum, Assessment and Reporting Authority, 2013) each state and territory education department offers strategies and guidelines catering to individual needs of GT students. The multivariate approach applied to gifted music education should draw on objective and subjective strategies for entry to specialist music schools – however, a performance audition is primarily subjective and dominates the process. Presented in my poster is a case for inclusion of objective aural test measures to identify, select and place primary school leavers for high stakes music education contexts.
Reported are initial findings from research involving participant applicants (N=73) to a specialist music secondary school in Sydney, Australia, investigating relations between objective measures of music aptitude (potential) and music literacy (attainment) as tested during the audition process in August 2013 using Gordon's Advanced Measures of Music Audiation (AMMA 1989) and Gordon's Iowa Test of Music Literacy Level 5 (ITML 1970, rev. 1991). Additionally a determination of the impact of intervention through a post test of Gordon's ITML Level 6 was conducted in August 2014. Results indicate positive and strong relationships between aptitude and attainment as measures gained objectively though Gordon's AMMA and ITML Level 5 by the applicant cohort. Results also indicate gains of high percentiles in Gordon's Level 5 that are maintained for Level 6 by the selected cohort (N=25), six months after entry. Inlcusion of objective measures of music aptitude enriches the audition process provides a balanced profile for gifts to talents in music.

Laura Danelli (University of Milano-Bicocca)

## Effects of Music Training on Reading and Memory in Preadolescence

Music education seems to facilitate the acquisition of cognitive and academic abilities. The reason for this association may lie in the intrinsic complexity of musical training. The ability to maintain prolonged controlled attention, to keep musical passages in working memory or to encode them into long-term memory, to decode music scores, and translate them into motor commands are fundamental skills for musicians. However, the majority of studies that reported an association between formal music training and cognitive ability are retrospective in nature. To investigate the effect of music training on cognitive development and in particular on reading and memory abilities, we performed a longitudinal study on fifty normally developing Italian students: The students were tested at the beginning of the sixth-grade, and at the beginning of the seventh-grade. Among these students, 35 were attending an educational program with intensive music training, 15 a canonical curriculum in which there was extra-training in topics not involving music. Three different working memory tests were administered to each participant: digit span forward, digit span backward, Corsi span, and the recall of a short-story, while reading abilities were evaluated by means of word, pseudo-word, and story reading tests. While both groups showed an increased performance in the Corsi span test and in the reading tasks, only the students attending the music training improved in their performance at the other memory tasks suggesting an association between intensive music education and specific components of working memory and verbal long-term memory.

Rosetta Dingle (South Carolina State University)

## Linking for Synergy: Music +

From the 1838 inception of music in schools of the United States of America, music curricula have been major points of discussion. Such discussions, among others, have centered on 'how', 'when' and 'what' skills and content are to be taught. Given political or social trends, music educators, researchers, and advocates simultaneously reported justifications and/or benefits of music in schools. Consequently, arts integration models emerged in regards to maintaining the integrity of music. This has been a recurring theme that appears to have been heard based on the U.S.A. federal *Elementary and Secondary Education* (ESEA) reauthorization act, recently passed into law (2015). The reauthorized act of ESSA includes music as a stand-alone, core academic subject necessary for a well-rounded education of students. The act provides an interesting platform for charting new directions of teaching learning-strategies. One such strategy is the idea of linking courses. According to Soven et al. (2013), linking may be defined as a type of learning-community-strategy whereby two courses are linked. Although designed for use in college courses, the concept may be used with general music at the elementary level. Linking general music with another subject may enrich elementary students' understanding of both subjects. Via collaboration, instructors of linked courses may identify salient, common concepts to be approached in a manner such that authentic or real-life knowledge, skills, and experiences evolve. In this way, additional learning experiences and skills may emerge. Therefore, the purpose of this paper is to explore the linking of general music and reading via a review of integrative literature. The presenter will also provide supporting evidence for implications of linking or pairing general music with another subject. Specific implications to be emphasized include (1) the acquisition of supplementary knowledge and skills and (2) improved student achievement.

**Józsefné Dombi (University of Szeged / Juhász Gyula Faculty of Education)**

## Famous Composers in Hungarian Music Education and the Culture of Szeged

2017 will commemorate the 135th anniversary of Zoltán Kodály and the 100th anniversary of György Ránki. We can celebrate their pieces during the anniversary events. Besides these famous composers there are lots of new talented composers that are of great importance for children's music. The aim of this poster is to present teaching material by famous composers: Zoltán Kodály (1882–1967), Béla Bartók (1881–1945), György Ránki (1907–1992) and contemporary composers such as György Kurtág (1926), Máté Hollós (1954), László Sáry (1940), Lajos Bárdos (1899–1986), Erzsébet Szőnyi (1924) and Miklós Kocsár (1933) which are appropriate for school education. In an analysis of new course books our questions were: At what point in their studies should students be introduced to the compositions of Kodály, Bartók, Ránki and those of contemporary composers? What methods are used in books? To what extent can new approaches foster a better understanding of works? How can an interdisciplinary approach be provided? Should/do the students have the possibility to take part in non-formal learning to listen to contemporary music of the Szeged Culture? We have found that the art of Béla Bartók and Zoltán Kodály receives special emphasis in the material of Hungarian school books. 20th century material and contemporary music are detailed in the textbooks for 7th and 8th graders and for secondary school 2nd graders. We examine the possibilities for students to participate and enjoy contemporary music in Szeged. It is a rewarding activity to take part in the "Youth Singing Festival" and in the "Fairy Tale Music". The new pieces to be presented are *Prince Árgyélus*, a children-opera by Péter Tóth and *Hansel und Gretel*, a music-tale by Ilona Dobszay-Meskó and Győző Lukácsházi. In our research we have come to the conclusion that Hungarian course books are informative about the composer, and use several different methods; however non-formal learning activities better stimulate students, and give students positive experiences.

**Miroslaw Dymon (University of Rzeszow)**

## After-School-Centers and Institutions as a Complement to Music Education

After-school-care-programs are an integral part of the Polish education system. These include: youth centers, houses of culture, and interschool sports centers. The main task is to conduct various forms of extracurricular activities that develop the capacity and interest of the students through organized spare time, preparing them to participate in a broad cultural life. In 1999 the change in the financing of education resulted in a drastic elimination of extracurricular activities. The biggest achievement of education institutions were the after-school-programs, developed during the years 1970 to 1980. In 1980, there were 600 in Poland, designed for the use of 450 thousand children and young people. Since then, the number of these entities systematically diminished due to financial reasons. Currently in the Podkarpackie province, eight institutions remain. The most popular activities among children and young people were musical activities. The poster will discuss, in how far the developments mentioned above affected the level of interest in and the perception of music among children and adolescents.

Andrea Gande (University of Music and Performing Arts, Graz) /
Silke Kruse-Weber (University of Music and Performing Arts, Graz)

## Instrumental Pedagogy in a Social Context: The Project "Meet4Music"

Within the current professional discourse in instrumental pedagogy, ways of opening up traditional learning contexts are being intensely discussed. Music-making at formal institutions is a rather exclusive activity, given the fact that one-to-one-tuition and the aspiration for excellence are omnipresent, keeping out people who do not belong to this 'artistic elite'. A further challenge for instrumental music education lies within demographic changes (e. g. the refugee crisis) which raise the question how pedagogues can answer new needs and address extremely heterogeneous and intercultural audiences. The focus is shifting to equity and participation. There is a need for concepts which allow learners to discover and develop their musical potential, whereas the emphasis lies on collaborative learning processes embedded in social contexts. How can an institution, e. g. a university, offer a low-threshold approach, so that all parts of society can actively take part in music-making and express themselves musically? The Institute of Music Education at Graz University of Music and Performing Arts dealt with this question by establishing "Meet4Music" in March 2016 – an open ensemble instructed by experts for choir, dance, theatre, percussion and Gamelan. The project's main goal is to offer people of all ages and socio-cultural backgrounds (including citizens of Graz, refugees and students) the opportunity to communicate lively through music and socialize with other group members, since neither previous knowledge nor registrations are needed to participate in the weekly events. Additionally university students of all departments can pick up "Meet4Music" as an elective course to foster their pedagogical competencies. The submitted poster outlines the specific facets of "Meet4Music" and describes the process of facilitating the ensemble and the facilitators' core competencies by analyzing guideline-based interviews with the experts. Also the possible benefits for both classically trained university students and ensemble participants from all socio-cultural backgrounds are being critically reflected.

Rita Ghosn (AFEM, France)

## Mapping for Singing (MfS) in the Classroom: "The Arlequin Interactive Listening and Learning Programme" (AILL)

MfS is a new pedagogical approach designed to stimulate and nurture an ear for music and a desire to perform in children aged seven to eleven. This workshop aims to initiate primary class teachers in the approach and promote musical awareness through active listening and singing. MfS uses the following interlinked tools and techniques:

- a new graphic musical language with mapping to enable children in the classroom to understand, memorize and 'learn' music,
- extracts from a participatory fairytale opera written for a young audience, with an original score and libretto featuring themes from popular classical arias revisited by the composer-librettist,
- one MfS singing exercise guide per aria.

The objectives of this method are:

- to stimulate active listening,
- to familiarize the child with popular classical melodies,
- to impart the key musical elements for understanding and using the graphic language,
- to encourage free expression,
- to foster in the child, through mapping, an ability to read and perform, to keep time and to create and colour his/her own sound maps.

Tools used in this context are:

- an illustrated booklet and CD presenting the story and ten melodies,
- MfS exercise cards for reading, creating and performing maps,
- pre-perforated maps for a mechanical music box.

The following process aims at getting the child involved:

- Draw the child into the story, sequence by sequence, through visual illustrations, narration and sound.
- Draw on his/her cognitive knowledge – alphabet, colours, familiar sounds for assimilation of MfS mapping
- Involve him/her by stimulating wonder, play and imagination through parody, surprises, guessing games, magic words...

Opening the ears and stimulating the mind – MfS offers an enjoyable introduction to the language of music, nurturing the music-lover in each child and democratizing access for all.

**Amelia Golema (Academy of Music, Wrocław)**

## Public Music Schools, General Public Schools and Home: Young adolescents Torn between Three Different Spheres

Children who attend a music school and public school could have assimilation problems. Quite frequently they refer to 'a life in two different worlds'. The influence of two schools, especially two peer groups, may be a real challenge for young people. In this situation, home as a 'place of prevention', sometimes assuming a therapeutic function, should be a place, where a child can be him- or herself and can find his/her 'real' personality. A parent's role and support is invaluable. First of all – by listening to their children, and offering adequate possibilities for dialogue and communication in general. But are parents really able to come up to these expectations? Interviews, which were conducted in public music schools in Poland (Wrocław), showed that parents often do not understand their children, and even if they want to help them, they don't know how to do it. Children expect their home to be a place, where they find a perspective mediating between their experiences in different schools.
This presentation is an attempt to answer following questions:

- What are essential requirements from a child's perspective?
- What problems occur for children exposed to the atmosphere of different schools and their parents?
- Can home be referred to as an 'ideal institution' for children? What needs should it satisfy?
- How can a good cooperation between public music schools, general public schools and home be established?

**Beate Hennenberg (University of Music and Performing Art Vienna)**

## Creative Music Making with Senior Citizens in a Day Center

Much has been written about, and a lot of research has been undertaken into music making in the formal context of music schools. However, creative music making in other institutions and in less formal settings is still considered to be at the edge of the young discipline of musical education. Socio-political developments of recent years have led to the belief that a wider view of the 'less-researched' contexts in which musical education takes place needs to be undertaken.
Work with heterogeneous groups provides a means of entry into the world of creative, musical education. Projects in this context may involve professional musicians well prepared to work together with amateurs, or groups where both able bodied and people with physical or mental impairments make music together. At the same time, with increasing opportunities to work in social fields the music profession as such and its marketing opportunities have changed. Concert halls and major festivals have lost some of their significance (Smilde/Alheit/Page 2015).
Different approaches are needed. Nothing is more damaging when working with the elderly than a performance-based approach to music making (Hartogh/Winding 2008). Our research project aims to demonstrate whether, and to what extent, the access to music making during the music units has an immediate impact on the visitors to the day centre. It also describes how authentic the students found the experience. For the project students planned music units, which included improvisation with rhythm instruments and sonification of visual images, they were then involved in the processes of preparation and the actual music making, offered guidance both in an ensemble and individually. They observed the participants and put down activities and personal impressions in seminar diaries.

**Birgit Huber (München)**

## "Coordination Centre for Music in Bavaria" (CCM)

The "Coordination Centre for Music in Bavaria" (CCM) [Bayerische Landeskoordinierungsstelle Musik / BLMK] serves as the center for music education projects in Bavaria. It was initiated by and works for the Bavarian Ministry of Education, Science and the Arts, the Bavarian State Ministry for Labor and Social Affairs, Family and Integration and the Bavarian Music Council. The CCM develops, carries out, accompanies and evaluates music projects for all age-groups.
The following aspects play an essential role for successful and sustainable school cooperation projects with public and private cultural institutions:

- close cooperation with the single school,
- mutual agreement about the educational goals,

- development of a common approach,
- mutual appreciation,
- evaluation of the projects.

Typical examples of cooperations are choir/choral classes, string classes, wind instrument classes, live music experiences with cultural institutions.

Before a project starts, the following aspects have to be considered:

- qualitative assessment of the external offers (e.g. qualification of external staff),
- financing (personnel and non-personnel costs),
- contract modalities between the partners.

**Evangelia Kopsalido (Democritus University of Thrace, Alexandroupolis)**

## Teaching Music in North-Eastern Greece (Thrace)

The geopolitical location as well as the historical circumstances of Greece at the time, have transformed the country into a meeting point for European, Northern African and Middle-Eastern cultures. Fables, beliefs and religious ceremonies, linguistic elements, traditional dances and music of different regions of the Hellenic sphere of influence testify this cultural convergence. One of these regions is Thrace which extends in the north-eastern part of the country and borders on Bulgaria in the North and Turkey in the East. The aim of this paper is to deal with music teaching in schools and universities of modern Thrace, a multicultural region, home to Turkish, Armenian, Russian, Albanian etc. minorities. Is music really an international language for them? Does it help them to integrate more easily in Greek society and to develop a better relationship with Greek pupils and students? Do they prefer music lessons to other lessons or ways of integration? In a detailed investigation into music lessons in schools and university departments of Thrace we are going to deal with these questions. We are going to present teaching examples (songs, creative proceedings, interdisciplinary approaches, music listening) in primary school and in two educational departments of Thrace (pre-school and primary school education) as well as in seminars for teachers from different cultural environments. All three institutions comprise pupils and students of different origins. They all speak Greek with a few exceptions. They all cooperate and communicate better with each other during music lessons. Most of them (pupils and students of minorities) prefer music to other lessons as a way of better understanding the Greek language, customs and people. The same is true for Greek pupils and students confronted with the culture of the minorities. Moreover, we will study the influence of these different 'music traditions' on human behavior and the everyday life of pupils and students who despite their different national origins are harmoniously sharing Thrace, eliminating the possibility of national conflicts. We will prove that while working together 'musically', They do not only respect each other, but they exchange characteristics of their respective cultures (expressions, songs, recipes, forms of entertainment).

**Barry Lee (The Education University of Hong Kong)**

## Networking for Music Education in Hong Kong: A Contextual Study of Stake-Holding Bodies Supporting School Music Teachers

Since the return of sovereignty to China in 1997, school music education in Hong Kong has been gradually transforming from a typical British (essentially westernized) model towards a locally-oriented music program which is both responsive to globalism and reflective of nationalism. Coupled with the implementation of the new music curriculum in school education, music education stake-holding bodies in Hong Kong have also been evolving in response to the contextual changes. This paper aims to investigate (1) the function of the music education associated stake-holding bodies in Hong Kong, (2) the extent that school music education is being supported by these stake-holding bodies, and (3) the current state of music education networking in Hong Kong. A comprehensive study of related documents and literature was conducted on the basis of the aims of investigation. The contextual elements associated with stake-holding bodies' involvement in school music education in Hong Kong were examined and analysed. Findings revealed each of the related stake-holding bodies played an active, important and meaningful role in complementing and supporting school music education in Hong Kong. However, the majority of these bodies were working in isolation with only limited coordination or collaboration, and issues such as works overlapping, support coverage and resources efficiency eventually arose. These observations reflected that the current state of music education networking in Hong Kong appears to be too loose. To optimize support given to schools and music teachers, a more organized and centralized network structure needs to be established to facilitate coordination, communication, collaboration and cooperation between schools and the stake-holding bodies, and to promote and encourage partnerships between different parties.

**Sezen Özeke (Uludağ University)**

## "Music Together®" Program: An Example of Early Childhood Music Education Model and its Effects on the Development of Children

Children learn through games, imitation, and modelling and they acquire most of their learning experiences through their environment and interactions with adults and with other children. A child's most intense learning experience happens during the period between birth and his/her sixth anniversary, during the so called early childhood or preschool period. The abilities that can be gained in this period are considered to be of particular importance for a child's healthy growth.

An awareness for the great significance of getting engaged in music and musical activities during this period has developed and inspired research. The effectiveness of music during this period is analyzed with regard to children's musical skills as well as non-musical skills. Musical activities are employed so as to support children's physical, cognitive, social and emotional development and the mastery of language during this early childhood period.

The program called "Music Together®", widely used in the United States and many other countries since 1987, will be discussed in my study aiming to provide variety of musical skills for children. Music Together®, basically a music-based program, emphasizes the importance of a participation of families and caregivers in the learning process. In this context, a special program allows children to model their families with the help of games.

The objectives, the philosophy and implementation of the "Music Together®" program will be presented, mentioning the importance of supporting a music enriched environment in early childhood and considering the impact of interactions within the family that help children to develop both from a musical and 'non-musical' perspective.

**Wolfgang Pfeiffer (Friedrich Alexander University Erlangen Nürnberg)**

## ‚Klasse.im.puls': Cooperation and Networking as a Multi-Layered Model of Working with Music Classes

The establishment of music classes at Bavarian schools is supported by Friedrich Alexander University Erlangen Nürnberg in cooperation with the Ministry of Education and Cultural Affairs. As a result, the active participation in making music is moved to the centre of regular music lessons. Music teachers, who are the link between schools and university, function as project managers and support schools in putting their projects into practice by giving teachers pieces of advice and tuition. After a project duration of six years, 180 Bavarian schools with a total of 400 music classes have participated in the project.

Various forms of the project have been established in this time:

- Model for newcomers: establishment of a music class (choir, band, winds and brass, strings, percussion, keyboard, orchestra) from the 5th class onwards. The introduction at schools is supported by project managers who offer their experience as experts to schools.
- Forum for already installied music classes: setting up a network of active schools for making the valuable experiences available to a circle of experts. All members of the network make their methods, forms of organization and their notes available to each other.
- Join concerts: Concerts with professional orchestras should give students further motivation. There they are able to work on a artistic project with persons of kindred spirit. The cooperation with professional musicians and technicians makes mutual learning possible. Students and their teachers gain an insight into professional music-making.

Cooperation and setting up the network takes place at the following levels:

- pupils' level: cooperation as a part of musical work; cooperation within different ensembles, which have to organize themselves at rehearsals and gigs;
- students' level: methods of teaching music classes as a content of studies; work placements in different schools with different models; cooperation with teachers within a model,

- teachers' level: cooperation with colleagues, teachers at music schools, students, musicians in an orchestra, music clubs, musisicians;
- music class level: exchange of ideas in forum; further education, joint events, quality management;
- organizational level: cooperation with orchestras, music schools, private music teachers, sound engineers, including parents as partners of cooperation at musical projects.

**Matteo Ricciardi (IA/Unicamp Campinas, Brazil) & Rita Addessi (University of Bologna)**

## Music Education in Compulsory Schools in Brazil and Italy: A Comparative Approach

The poster presents the partial results of a PhD research in music in progress, which discusses the musical teacher training profile in Brazil and Italy. In this specific proposal, the poster refers to a comparative study of historical aspects regarding the presence of music education in the school system law for primary education in both countries. In Brazil, the educational legislation has contained the arts as subject in the curriculum of primary schools since its enactment in 1996 (9.394/96), and in 2008 another specific law (11.769/08) reinforced the compulsory presence of music as a curriculum component. The proposal for operationalization of this law newly published (Resolution 2 of May 10, 2016) marks a step towards the implementation and the development of the Common National Base Curriculum and adds new perspectives to the discussion. In Italy, music education appeared in secondary school programs in 1979 (D.M. 9/1979) and for primary education it was taken up in 1985 (D.P.R. 12/1985), and the legislative aspects have been affected by specific indications in the curricula indications for primary and first level secondary schools in 2012 (D.M. 254/2012). Methodologically this study aims at performing a content analysis (cmp. Bardin, 2011) of official documents. The focus is on the question how the curriculum component 'music' is understood in official texts of the respective countries in order to identify possible mutual trends and contributions.

**Steven Schiemann (University of Education Freiburg)**

## Professionalizing Generalist Primary Teachers to Teach Music

Generalist primary music teachers cover up to 80 % of all of music lessons taught in primary schools (Hammel, 2011). To professionalize generalist primary music teachers, who usually have little to no prior musical background in (teaching) music, this practice-based research project was conducted. The aim of this study was to describe changes in the generalist primary music teachers' didactic classroom practices in teaching music. Moreover, this study aimed to analyze the generalist primary music teachers' development of their 'musical self-concept' (Spychiger, 2010) and factors concerning motivation in music teaching (Harnischmacher & Hörtschz, 2012). This longitudinal intervention study is qualitative in character. Participants were eight generalist primary music teachers and four specialist primary music teachers (control group). The generalist primary music teachers were divided into two groups. The first group (n=4) received four coaching sessions (group 1), the second group (n=4) received four coaching sessions and 56 hours of further education in music didactics (group 2) for one schoolyear. The control group received no special treatment. The individual coaching sessions for all generalist primary music teachers (group 1 and 2) followed the 'Content Focused Coaching' (CFC) concept. Empirical data were collected before the beginning and at the end of the study by video-observations of classroom performances in primary music lessons (n=24), and questionnaires concerning the teachers 'musical self-concepts' and their motivation (n=24). The findings suggest on the one hand that generalist music teachers require fairly little support to enhance their didactic performance of teaching music in primary music lessons. But on the other hand it appears that coaching without a parallel measure of further education seems to be to no avail for the group of less musically trained generalist music teachers.

**Motje Wolf (De Montfort University Leicester) / David Holland (De Montfort University Leicester) / Jack Richardson (De Montfort University Leicester)**

## Fostering Creative Engagement with Sound-Based Music

This paper introduces research conducted in the "Music, Technology & Innovation Research Centre" and the "Education Division" at De Montfort University (UK) focussing on sound-based music in schools. We will present key studies that we conducted over the last decade. The associated research projects have developed a curriculum for sound-based music, teaching strategies for the development of listening strategies, teacher training initiatives, a model of teacher CPD and an online learning environment that is free to be used in schools (http://ears2.dmu.ac.uk). We will present a synthesis of the key findings, for example that the appreciation of and engagement with sound-based music has to rely on the development of listening strategies. In our research, we worked with pupils of different age groups and teachers in different school types. We will introduce these strategies and discuss the meaning of our findings within the school context.

**Cheng Xie (University of Music and Performing Arts Munich)**

## Traces of "Rhythmic Musical Education" from Germany to China

Rhythmical-musical education in Germany looks back on more than 100 years of history. It has been developed into a holistic pedagogical concept. In my research, supported by the Chinese Ministry of Education as a research project of the "China Scholarship Council" (CSC) I do not only reflect about the development of rhythmicity in the German-speaking world, but also about the current state of rhythmicity in China. My approach focuses on a cultural sensitive aspect of rhythmical musical education. It is based on the evaluation of expert interviews in China. So the special pedagogical needs of China can be taken into account for a further development of Eurhythmics. Three aspects will be discussed in my poster-presentation:

(1) Émile Jaques-Dalcroze, the founder of rhythmicity, taught important pupils. Mimi Scheiblauer found possible applications in therapeutic education. Elfriede Feudel and Charlotte Pfeiffer put forth their efforts at establishing Eurhythmics as a scientific university subject. In German-speaking countries, important people, such as Karl Lorenz, Eleonore Witoszynsky, Rudolf Konrad, are involved in the further development of rhythmicity. A new generation of rhythmists from different countries has set itself the task to set its own accents. In this context the Chinese perspective will be considered. The conceptual world of Jaques-Dalcroze can easily be connected with Chinese philosophy. This becomes most evident in the use of the YinYang symbol in the conception of buildings for the Institute of Hellerau.

(2) An important development of rhythmic-musical education is known in China as "New System". It was established by Professor Gao Jianjin of the Central Conservatory of Music. "New System" includes thoughts of Jaques-Dalcroze, Carl Orff and Zoltán Kodály.

(3) In the future, a culture-sensitive approach is considered necessary. The most important aspects of this approach will be presented.

**Nikolaos Zafranas (Aristotle University of Thessaloniki)**

## Musical Exploration in Piano Teaching: Gaining a Deeper Understanding of the Relationship between Student and Teacher

Music, as an interactive social phenomenon, requires a responsive and receptive disposition to both the student and the musical material. This is true for the process of teaching a musical instrument (Malloch & Trevarthen, 2009). According to Custodero (2003), if content knowledge cannot be communicated in a meaningful way, approaches are useless at best and possibly dangerous. Obviously dispositions toward lifelong learning are established early and can lead to musical/non-musical identity formation. It might be necessary to reconsider the emphasis of piano teaching placing a much larger weight on the student-teacher relationship, a notion supported by Elliot & Silverman (2014) in their description of musical performance as a live deployment of one's whole self where the musician deploys thinking-in-action, knowing-in-action and reflecting-in-action. Interdisciplinary research has shown an expansion of the flow and effectiveness produced by music lesson thanks to the awareness of communication processes (Psaltopoulou et al., 2014; 2015).

The main aim of this study was to investigate how the awareness of music teaching communication processes affected the teacher-student relationship with regard to the corresponding musical outcome. The study was conducted with 17 young adult students in private individual piano lessons, groups and music school settings in Greece, 2015. Qualitative analysis through content analysis of videotaped piano lessons was selected to capture the essence of the teacher-student relationships.

The analysis comprised three stages: coding conceptual classification of the data in categories; verification by three other independent researchers; outcome of conclusions from findings. Results show that teachers' and students' awareness improves musical understanding and production. The findings are presented so as to reveal common areas, which all participants found to be true for themselves. This approach combines the focus on the piano student and the student-teacher relationship with the use of Lacan's four types of discourse (1998) as tools to improve both musical effectiveness and well-being in the piano lesson.

# CONCERT PROGRAMS

## OPENING CEREMONY

Welcome addresses by Dr. Wilfried Haslauer (Governor of the Federal Province of Salzburg), Dr. Heinz Schaden (Mayor of Salzburg), Sarah Wedl-Wilson, MA (Deputy-Chancellor of Mozarteum University Salzburg), Prof. Lee Higgins (President of ISME), Prof. Dr. Gerhard Sammer (EAS President), Prof. Dr. Monika Oebelsberger (Head of the Department for Music Pedagogy at Mozarteum University Salzburg).

## (IM) POSSIBLE MUSIC

**Andreas Martin Hofmeir's Tuba Class meets the Recorder Students of Dorothee Oberlinger**

### Andreas Martin Hofmeir and his Tuba-Class of Mozarteum University Salzburg

©Philippe Gerlach

Cut down the borders in your mind: The border between classical and pop music as well as the border between two instruments which couldn't be more different. The recorder, an instrument for small kids, the tuba, an instrument for overweight men. Be honest: Did we 'catch' your thoughts???
This performance will play with your prejudice – and may change a lot.

### Recorder-Consort of Mozarteum University

©Privat

The Recorder Consort is an ensemble consisting of students working with Dorothee Oberlinger. Different recorders – from the small descant recorder to the great bass recorder - are played and the Consort specialises in interpreting pieces of the 16th century and beginning of the 17th century. Since 2015, the ensemble gives concerts at home and abroad regularly, for example at the Baroque festival in Bad Arolsen, and takes part in workshops.

**Thursday, 20 April 2017, Solitär of Mozarteum University**

# A YOUNG PERSONS' GUIDE TO MUSIC COMPOSED IN SALZBURG

**Concert of Students of Salzburg Pre-College**

Heinrich Ignaz Franz Biber
(1644–1704)

Passacaglia in G-minor from the *Mystery Sonatas* for Violin solo (1676)
Theresa Giehl, Violin / Class: Brigitte Schmid

Cesar Bresgen
(1913–1988)

*Five Miniatures for Flute and Guitar* (1979)
Julia Klampfer, Flute / Class: Britta Bauer
Gyöngyi Bartha, Guitar / Class: Maria Isabel Siewers de Pazur

Wolfgang Amadé Mozart
(1756–1791)

Rondo in D-major for Flute and Orchestra KV Anh. 184 (1781)
Fabian Egger, Flute / Class: Britta Bauer
Florian Podgoreanu, Piano

Wolfgang Amadé Mozart
(1756–1791)

Allegretto grazioso from Rondo in C-major
for Violin and Orchestra KV 373 (1781)
Lilli Schneider, Violin / Class: Wonji Kim
Patrick Leung, Piano

Anton Diabelli
(1781–1858)

Second Menuett from Serenade for Flute, Viola and Guitar op. 95 (1818)
Paula Riedler, Flute / Class: Britta Bauer
Riana Heath, Viola / Class: Wonji Kim
Gyöngyi Bartha, Guitar / Class: Maria Isabel Siewers de Pazur

Jakob Gruchmann
(*1991)

Monodie and Monolog from *Three Monofonien* for Flute Solo (2014)
Julia Klampfer, Flute / Class: Britta Bauer

Heinrich Ignaz Franz Biber
(1644–1704)

Partita in G-minor for two Violins and Basso continuo (1696)
Intrada: Alla breve
Aria: Adagio
Balletto: Presto
Gigue
Passacaglia: Adagio / Allegro / Adagio
Magdalena Waldauf, Violin / Class: Klara Flieder
Laura-Maria Waldauf, Violin / Class: Esther Hoppe
Hanna Giehl, Violoncello / Class: Barbara Lübke
N.N., Harpsichord

Wolfgang Amadé Mozart
(1756–1791)

Allegro from the Violin Concerto in D-major KV 218 (1775)
Yohei Shimizu, Violin / Class: Wonji Kim
Atsuko Shimizu, Piano

*GCC – Guided Collective Composition* – world premiere (2017)
Composition project of all young students of the composition classes in the Pre-College Salzburg
Susila Heath, Violin
Irina Schukoff, Violoncello
Kalina Ciesielczyk, Piano
Class: Ludwig Nussbichler

## Salzburg Pre-College

In keeping with the aims of finding and encouraging young talent, the Salzburg Pre-College seeks to register gifted musicians at an early age and to encourage them in the best possible way, both in the central artistic subject as well as in a broad musical context, and to guide them towards a later artistic career. Besides training highly gifted young musicians, greater attention is to be given to their special inclinations, for instance, for improvisation, composition etc. These preferences can be particularly encouraged by relevant subject matter from the range of available teaching courses. The Mozarteum University Salzburg bears substantial responsibility for providing the framework conditions of a pre-university training for its future students by accepting outstandingly talented pupils in the Salzburg Pre-College. This applies in particular for instrumental studies in which early intensive training is, as we know from experience, essential in order to fully explore the potential for achievement.

# LUNCH CONCERTS

## BORG Gastein Chor & Band (BORG Bad Hofgastein)

©ORF / Milenko Badzic

The BORG Gastein is an acclaimed high school for students aged 14 to 18, with a special focus on music, art and creativity. Besides graduating with an A-level equivalent after four years, the pupils are also highly educated in the performing arts, trained on various musical instruments, and in singing and dancing; plus they are offered additional courses in multi-media art, sound engineering, playing in a band, stage lighting and acting.

The school's elite choir excels in performing assorted pop songs, featuring talented soloists backed up by the well-known BORG school band. The choir was awarded First Prize in the national music competition "Falco goes School" by the Falco Foundation Vienna in 2016, and achieved third place on Austria's famous TV show "Die große Chance der Chöre" in 2015.

These enthusiastic young performers have, through their many appearances and shared experiences, transformed themselves into a strong and powerful performing entity. They have one clear goal: to spread the joy and pleasure of making great live music together.

Performers: Choir & Band of BORG Gastein
Conductor: Elisabeth Wieland

## danceLABmusgym (Musisches Gymnasium Salzburg)

©Paul Rehrl

Every year, about 1000 students of the Salzburg Musical Gymnasium between the ages of ten and eighteen assemble, choosing an individualized curriculum depending on their preferences in music, arts, theatre, dance and creative writing. On average, 200 of them decide on expanding their knowledge of creative dance.

Our program is based on Rudolf von Laban's idea of community-based dance, and gives the students the opportunity to develop technical, creative and performance skills. Besides the creative and practical aspects of the curriculum, we also discuss the understanding of the arts in contexts, and aim to improve students' critical, analytical, and reflective skills. Our goal is to let students enrich their own capacity for movement observation, expand their movement vocabulary, embrace new strategies for dance composition, and develop a unique choreographic voice. Our students thoroughly enjoy the opportunity to perform, as well as create, unique works of dance. Our presentation for the lunch concert will be a show of their own works, as well as a backstage look at how these works were created.

Performers: danceLABmusgym
Head of department: Astrid Weger Purkhart

# CONFERENCE DINNER – MUSIC

## "Moz-Partie"

©Bernhard Strobl

Traditional Austrian Folkmusic has a long history as well as a bright future. At the Conference Dinner you can get an impression of the lively present. The group "Moz-Partie" acompanies that evening with typical Austrian music and instruments. All members of that ensemble are students of the Department for Music Pedagogics of Mozarteum University Salzburg.

# CLOSING CEREMONY CONCERT

## The BBB "Pluskurs Big Band" (Privatgymnasium Borromäum Salzburg)

©Anton Temmel

Founded in 2007 by Christoph Moser as a school-based big band, the Triple BBB (Big Band Borromäum) became a "Pluskurs" in 2014, a change which permitted open enrollment for every student who is interested in jazz, plays a traditional big-band instrument, and enjoys making music with their peers. At the moment, the members of the Triple BBB come from five different schools in Salzburg. In addition to the annual concert at local jazz club "Jazzit", the band has played concerts in Brixen and Milan, Italy. The BBB has also joined the autumn 2016 collaborative musical production of *The Blues Brothers* (created by the BAfEP, Borromäum, and Ursulinen) as a stage band! During its time in operation, the band has expanded its repertoire to include big band classics as well as funk, soul, and modern arrangements.

Performers: The BBB "Pluskurs Big Band"
Conductor: Christoph Moser

# ADDITIONAL PROGRAMME

**"Join in"**
The music teachers of some schools in the town of Salzburg kindly invite registered guests to listen to their music lessons. During those 'School Visits' you can gain insights into the Austrian school system.
Guests can choose between different types of schools with musical focus, e.g. Primary School (Volksschule der Franziskaner Salzburg, www.vs-franziskanerinnen.salzburg.at), Academic Secondary School (Privatgymnasium Borromäum Salzburg, www.borromaeum.at, Musisches Gymnasium Salzburg, www.musischesgymnasium.at) or a College for Higher Vocational Education (Private Bildungsanstalt für Elementarpädagogik Salzburg, www.bafep-salzburg.at).

**"Join us"**
on a walk following the traces of some Salzburgian Musicians. Our 'musical tour', accompanied by Salzburg musicians will take us to Salzburg Episcopal Church, St. Peter's and Mozart's Residence (Mozart Wohnhaus).

# MOZARTEUM UNIVERSITY SALZBURG – WHERE TALENT GROWS INTO EXCELLENCE

**Mozarteum University Salzburg – where talent grows into excellence.**
**Mozart is our inspiration, music our tradition, art our passion.**

**In the heart of Salzburg exceptional talents mature into artistic personalities – on the pulse of time, for the world's stages.**

**The cultural heritage of Europe forms the foundation on which we, an international community, promote liberal and tolerant dialogue, critically reflecting on the society we live in today.**

©Christian Schneider

The Mozarteum University offers over 40 artistic and education courses in the fields of music, the performing and visual arts. 1,500 young artists from all over the world experience comprehensive training here in all instruments, in composition, conducting, singing, music-theatre, acting, stage-directing, stage design, music and dance education, art and craft education as well as in music pedagogics and musicology.

500 lecturers, many of whom are internationally renowned artists and teachers, pass on their knowledge and their art, thus making the university a place of lively intellectual exchange and dialogue.

The history of the Mozarteum University goes back to the year 1841 and is characterised by the work and teaching of outstanding personalities such as Bernhard Paumgartner, Clemens Krauss, Paul Hindemith, Nikolaus Harnoncourt, Carl Orff and Sándor Végh. The Mozarteum School of Music was founded by the Salzburg Cathedral Music Association. In 1914 it became a conservatory, in 1953 an academy, in 1970 a Hochschule of music and performing arts and finally, in 1998, a university.

The Mozarteum University fosters international relations with associated music and art academies by means of an international exchange of lecturers and students, scholarship programmes, exchange concerts and mutual projects.

Students and lecturers engage in joint artistic activities as an integral part of the course programme. They perform in public in several concerts, plays, dance and opera productions as well as participating in exhibitions, thereby enriching cultural life in Salzburg. Besides intensive studies in an arts-friendly environment, networks are created here for later professional careers.

## Musikpädagogische Beiträge

Bernd Clausen

**Der Hase im Mond**

Studie zu japanischer Musik im japanischen Musikunterricht

Die vorliegende Arbeit geht der Frage nach, wie sich japanischer Musikunterricht gegenüber den an ihn implizit und explizit gestellten Forderungen nach Veränderung stellt. Der Fokus liegt dabei auf die Einbindung so genannter traditioneller japanischer Musik in den schulischen Musikunterricht. Diese Untersuchung besteht aus insgesamt drei Teilstudien, die in den Jahren 2005 und 2006 geplant und durchgeführt wurden.

(with an English and Japanese summary)

Bd. 8, 2009, 472 S., 39,90 €, br., ISBN 978-3-8258-1675-9

Christian Spatscheck; Markus Nachtigall; Robert Lehenherr; Wilfried Grüßinger

**HAPPY NATION?!?**

Jugendmusikkulturen und Jugendarbeit in den 90er Jahren

Jugend und ihre Musik – zwei Welten, die immer wieder Erstaunen und Überraschung, manchmal auch Unverständnis und Ablehnung auslösen. Nie war Jugendkultur so vielfältig, farbenfroh und widersprüchlich wie heute.

Dieses Buch gibt einen Einblick in die bis heute dominierenden musikalischen Strömungen „Hip Hop" und „Techno".

Zudem wird ausführlich auf die entscheidenden psycho-sozialen Bedeutungen von Jugendmusikkulturen für Jugendliche eingegangen. In einer Gesellschaft, die in ihrer Komplexität besonders für Jugendliche immer schwieriger zu durchschauen ist, bieten gerade solche jugendkulturellen Äußerungen eine Möglichkeit der Orientierung. Diese Zusammenhänge zu kennen ist nicht nur für pädagogische Dienstleister, sondern auch für Eltern interessant und wichtig.

Im zweiten Teil des Buches beschreiben die Autoren, welche Konsequenzen sich aus diesen Erkenntnissen für die Praxis ableiten lassen. Ausführlich beschrieben werden sechs erfolgreiche Projekte, die durch ihren Bezug zu den Musikstilen „Techno", „Hip Hop" oder „Rockmusik" zu innovativen Beispielen moderner Jugendarbeit geworden sind.

Bd. 6, 2. Aufl. 2008, 234 S., 15,90 €, br., ISBN 978-3-8258-3485-2

Ilse Storb

**Jazz und Neue Musik im Unterricht**

Jazz ist eine *vitale, kreative, befreiende und partnerschaftliche Musik!* Das vorliegende Buch ist didaktisch und methodisch bis ins Detail ausgearbeitet. Der *Nachholbedarf* auf dem Gebiet des Jazz und insbesondere der Jazzpädagogik ist in Deutschland sehr gross. Das hat mindestens 2 Gründe: 1. die "entartete Niggermusik" war während der *Nazi-Zeit* verboten. 2. Die traditionelle Musikwissenschaft ist immer noch weitgehend *eurozentrisch* eingestellt. – Die musikpädagogischen Ausbildungsstätten bemühen sich in letzter Zeit mehr und mehr um die Bereiche *Jazz/Rock/Pop.* – Das Buch umfasst die folgenden Teile:

*Systematische Aspekte:* Was ist Jazz? Jazzrhythmik, Jazzimprovisation, Jazztongebung

*Historische Aspekte:* Spiritual, Blues, Louis Armstrong, Duke Ellington, Charlie Parker, Miles Davis, Free Jazz, Rockjazz, Jazz und Neue Musik.

*Soziologische Aspekte:* Rassendiskriminierung, Bessie Smith, Billie Holiday.

Bd. 1 (mit CD), 2001, 136 S., 15,90 €, br., ISBN 3-8258-3755-6

LIT Verlag Berlin – Münster – Wien – Zürich – London

Auslieferung Deutschland / Österreich / Schweiz: siehe Impressumsseite